WITHDRAWN

HARVARD LIBRARY

WITHDRAWN

# HERMENEUTICAL STUDIES

*Dilthey, Sophocles and Plato*

Barrie A. Wilson

Problems in Contemporary Philosophy
Volume 25

The Edwin Mellen Press
Lewiston/Queenston/Lampeter

BD
241
.W52
1990

**Library of Congress Cataloging-in-Publication Data**

Wilson, Barrie A.
　Hermeneutical studies : Dilthey, Sophocles, and Plato / Barrie A. Wilson.
　　p.　cm. -- (Problems in contemporary philosophy ; v. 25)
　Includes bibliographical references.
　ISBN 0-88946-370-0
　1. Hermeneutics. 2. Bible--Hermeneutics. I. Title. II. Series.
BD241.W52　1990
121'.68--dc20　　　　　　　　　　　　　　　　　　　　　　90-34005
　　　　　　　　　　　　　　　　　　　　　　　　　　　　　　CIP

This is volume 25 in the continuing series
Problems in Contemporary Philosophy
Volume 25 ISBN 0-88946-370-0
PCP Series ISBN 0-88946-325-5

A CIP catalog record for this book
is available from the British Library.

Copyright © 1990 The Edwin Mellen Press

All rights reserved. For information contact

The Edwin Mellen Press　　　　　　The Edwin Mellen Press
Box 450　　　　　　　　　　　　　　　Box 67
Lewiston, New York　　　　　　　　Queenston, Ontario
USA 14092　　　　　　　　　　　　　CANADA L0S 1L0

The Edwin Mellen Press, Ltd.
Lampeter, Dyfed, Wales
UNITED KINGDOM SA48 7DY

Printed in the United States of America

# HERMENEUTICAL STUDIES

*Dilthey, Sophocles and Plato*

*for my parents*

*Marion Wilson*
*Andy Wilson*

## TABLE OF CONTENTS

Preface ........................................................................................... ix

Acknowledgements ........................................................................ xi

PART ONE: HERMENEUTICAL DIRECTIONS

    1. Interpretation: The One and the Many ............................... 3

PART TWO: HERMENEUTICAL CRITIQUES

    2. Dilthey's Dilemma .............................................................. 27

    3. Bultmann's Hermeneutics:
       A Critical Examination ....................................................... 59

    4. Hirsch's Hermeneutics:
       A Critical Examination ....................................................... 87

PART THREE: HERMENEUTIC STUDIES

    5. Plato: Some Inconsistencies ............................................. 117

    6. Bardaisan: On Nature, Fate, and Freedom ..................... 131

PART FOUR: A HERMENEUTICAL DIRECTION

    7. Interpretation, Meta-Interpretation
       and Sophocles' *Oedipus Tyrannus* ................................. 159

INDEX ......................................................................................... 209

# PREFACE

*HERMENEUTICAL STUDIES* represents a series of hermeneutic studies unified by two main concerns:

1. to sort out and reconcile the varying claims of the text and the interpreter's perspective, and

2. to urge reorientation of hermeneutic inquiry towards the study of types and patterns of interpretive arguments as reflected in sound interpretive practice.

The many strands of contemporary hermeneutic inquiry grow out of the dilemma posed by Dilthey around the turn of the 20th century. The studies I have initiated begin with that dilemma and, from that, branch off into a number of specific topics. In no sense, however, do they attempt to deal with all the current controversial issues in hermeneutics which include, at the minimum, the following kinds of investigations.

There are those who focus on the respective roles of different *people* involved in interpretation – the author, the initial audience, the interpreter, or the audience for whom the interpretation is intended. There are also those who emphasize the *relationships* involved, from writing a text to reading a text, as well as those who note the *contextual influence* of culture, tradition, and the surrounding circumstances within which the people involved in interpretation stand.

Others stress the *act of interpreting*, which is itself both creative as well as mediational. It is creative in the sense that it involves an imaginative awareness of the text and the audiences, both original as well as contemporary. It is mediational in that there is an onus on the interpreter to transmit something from the original to the contemporary audience. The extent to which this is possible, and the feasibility of this requirement, raises, of course, some of the most contentious issues in hermeneutics today. Some would describe these issues as phenomenological; others, as epistemological, or even moral in nature.

The problems become much more diffuse when what is interpreted varies. Texts vary by field as well as by genre, and, as a result, some have proposed differing hermeneutics. Dilthey proposed a hermeneutic for "cultural artefacts." Others have included actions, events, dances, living traditions, dreams, symbols, and other expressions of personal and cultural life.

I present these studies into selected aspects of hermeneutics partly in the hope that some clarification has been achieved, to urge the value of probing interpretive arguments as a much neglected area of hermeneutics, and to welcome others into the study of this fascinating problem area.

## ACKNOWLEDGEMENTS

I gratefully acknowledge the cooperation of the following in giving me permission to reprint material previously published.

"Interpretation, Meta-Interpretation, and Sophocles' *Oedipus The King*." Reprinted with permission; originally published in the protocol of the Thirty-ninth Colloquy, © copyright 1980 by the Center for Hermeneutical Studies, 2400 Ridge Rd., Berkeley CA 94709.

"Interpretation: The One and the Many." Originally published in *Queen's Quarterly*, 87 (1980), 16-30.

"Bardaisan: On Nature, Fate and Freedom" Reprinted with permission; originally published in *International Philosophical Quarterly* 24 (1984), 165-178.

"Hirsch's Hermeneutics: A Critical Examination." Reprinted with permission; originally published in *Philosophy Today* 22 (1978), 20-33.

"Bultmann's Hermeneutics: A Critical Examination." Reprinted by permission of Kluwer Academic Publishers. Originally published in *International Journal for Philosophy of Religion* 8 (1977), 169-189.

The articles on Dilthey and Plato have not previously been published.

A very special thanks to Rita Marinucci for word processing these articles, and especially to Hazel O'Loughlin for her expert eye and attention to detail in preparing the typeset version. Without their co-operation and commitment these articles would not have been so readily assembled.

# PART ONE:

# HERMENEUTIC DIRECTIONS

# CHAPTER 1

## INTERPRETATION: THE ONE AND THE MANY

In the last of his Four Quartets, T.S. Eliot wrote:

> *We shall not cease from exploration*
> *And the end of all our exploring*
> *Will be to arrive where we started*
> *And know the place for the first time.*

What does he mean? In his *Pattern and Meaning in History*, Wilhelm Dilthey, the German philosopher of culture, wrote: "Everywhere understanding opens up a world." What does he mean?

It is one thing to interpret a text; it is quite another matter, however, to offer an account of what constitutes textual interpretation. The former I shall call "interpretation;" the latter, "meta-interpretation." Interpretation seeks to make clear what a text means, its focus being upon the primary matter of understanding the text. Meta-interpretation, on the other hand, is concerned with the nature of textual interpretation. Its object is to clarify textual interpretation itself, thereby to understand textual understanding. What I call "meta-interpretation" has often been referred to as "hermeneutics."[1]

Interpretation and meta-interpretation are distinguishable, for what they are about differs and they raise different critical questions. Yet it should also be noted that they are closely linked. Interpretation, for instance, presupposes a meta-interpretive stance, whether consciously adopted or not, for otherwise the interpreter would not know for what he is looking. Similarly, meta-interpretation must be critically aware of interpretation if it is to offer a sound, comprehensive and satisfactory account of its nature.

With this terminology in mind, I propose to do three things in this article. First, I shall delineate some of the differences between interpretive and meta-interpretive questions. Apart from clarification, this will serve to illustrate some of the complexities involved in understanding, and more generally, in understanding understanding. Second, I shall critically examine various alternative solutions to one central meta-interpretive issue, the problem of the one and the many. Finally, and chiefly by way of concluding, I detect several important presuppositions which give rise to different conceptions of interpretation in the humanities.

Questions concerning the meaning of texts are familiar in all areas of the humanities. Philosophical, literary, religious, legal, and historical texts frequently pose difficult questions of interpretation. Examples are endless. How, for instance, should Plato's *Republic* be understood? Is it a work that negates human freedom, or is it rather one that portrays a model of a truly just society in which each member would experience the greatest degree of fulfilment possible? Is the Book of Daniel in the Bible a work of prophecy dating from the Babylonian Exile and referring to historical events in the far-distant future, or is it rather a work of comfort for the Hasidim composed during the reign of Antiochus Epiphanes? What does Shakespeare's *MacBeth* mean? Is it legitimate to give this play a Freudian, or a Marxist, or a feminist interpretation when its composition clearly predates these movements, or should it rather be construed strictly "on its own terms" (whatever that may indicate)?

Some examples of mulling over the meaning of texts are even more complicated. Genesis, for example, contains two accounts of creation (Genesis 1:1-2:25, the transition from one account to the other occurring in the middle of 2:4). These accounts, however, are incompatible. What, then, do these passages mean, assuming that the composer-compiler of Genesis could, like us, recognize incompatibility? Moreover, what can Aristotle possibly mean by the separability of the active intellect in *De Anima III*, 4 and 5 when in *De Anima*

*Interpretation: The One and the Many*

II, I he has explicitly said that the soul is not separable from the body? How is this inconsistency to be understood?

In addition, the Gospels in the New Testament, themselves highly edited documents of a pre-existing and creative oral tradition, present quite different pictures of the teaching of Jesus. Three of them (Mark, Matthew, Luke) present Jesus putting forth, largely in the form of parables, teachings concerning the Kingdom of God; on the other hand, John portrays Jesus as speaking chiefly about himself in terms of complex images (*e.g.*, Son of Man, Son of God, Bread of Life, Light of the World, Good Shepherd, the Resurrection, the True Vine) largely in monologue form. Even with respect to the former, much remains unclear. What, for instance, was the purpose of his parables: to mystify? to clarify? What is their literary type: allegory, metaphor or perhaps some other distinctive form? And how is it possible to differentiate strata in the editing process the Gospels underwent, so as clearly to distinguish the words of Jesus from the editorial contributions of the early church? In the light of these manifold interpretive problems, it is now a very complex matter to ascertain, on the basis of the extant documents, what Jesus taught.

We are often faced, then, with the situation of having to make sense of the meaning of a text. When we are uncertain what a text means, we ask: what does it mean? I shall refer to this question as "question A." In asking question A, we have asked a question that has to do with the interpretation of the work we are examining. Indeed, it is the fundamental question of interpretation. How one goes about answering question A is a difficult matter, especially in the more complex situations involving incompatibility, inconsistency, or both combined with an edited document, and particularly in the light of different schools of interpretation. In a sense these more complicated interpretive situations force a reflection on what it is the interpreter seeks to accomplish with respect to the text before him. They invite the interpreter to seek distance from the text and his interpretive activity and to ask a second but very different question: what is it to give an interpretation to a text? I shall refer to this question as "Question B." Question B is of a very different sort than question A: it is asked on a different theoretical level, for B is about the activity involved in answering A. It is a meta-interpretive kind of question.

Not everything that can be said about a text constitutes an interpretation of that text. In some fashion or other, giving an interpretation to a text needs to be distinguished from other text-related activities such as writing a commentary on a text, providing helpful background information for a text, giving a lecture or writing an essay on a text, adding a gloss or a few notes to a text, etc., which may or may not have much to do with the text's meaning. Important though this task of differentiation and clarification may be, I shall not tackle this meta-interpretive issue here.

It is important to note, moreover, that the pursuit of textual meaning is not a solitary one. With respect to any text we have occasion to interpret, we usually find that there is a considerable tradition of scholarly interpretation. Interpretation normally operates within a community of scholarship, one which often involves different "schools" or approaches to interpretation. In all areas of the humanities, texts have been written about texts in the attempt to make clear the meaning of the original texts and to put their significance and importance into context. Often, of course, there is very little consensus concerning the meaning of particular texts. Indeed the range of interpretive diversity is occasionally quite startling.[2]

When confronted by several quite different interpretations of a text we are studying, we may very well find ourselves asking: well, should all these different interpretations of a text be reconciled? If so, how? How do these different interpretations relate? Are they all true, all equally acceptable? Or all false? Or, perhaps, is only one true? If so, which one? And how do I tell? And so on. The situation of interpretive diversity raises a number of critical questions such as these. Generally, they all have to do with the fundamental question: how do

# Interpretation: The One and the Many

different conflicting interpretations of a text relate to each other? I shall refer to this question as "question C." In asking question C we are again asking a question which is about the meaning of a text. It is, therefore, a meta-interpretive question, and it raises many complicated meta-interpretive issues, one of them being the problem of the one and the many. It is to this problem that I now turn.

The problem is this. On the one hand, should texts be construed as having one and only one correct interpretation? This approach is known as "the single sense approach." Simply stated it is the view that texts ought to be regarded as having one and only one correct interpretation (one correct sense). So, on this approach, when we answer question A we should attempt to find its one correct interpretation. Likewise, for question C, we should say, "yes, different interpretations of a text ought to be reconciled: there cannot be several equally good interpretations of a text.".

On the other hand, should texts be regarded as having many different interpretations? This approach may be referred to as "the multiple sense approach." Simply stated this is the view that texts should be regarded as having a variety of equally legitimate interpretations (or senses). So, on this approach, when we answer question A, we would expect to find a multiplicity of interpretations. Likewise, for question C, we would not expect different interpretations of a text to be reconciled: in fact, we would expect divergent diversity.

The problem of the one and the many has been a major controversy in the study of the humanities over the centuries. The views are quite different, for they involve different views concerning the nature of textual interpretation and the nature of the humanities. They involve, moreover, different views of the sort of knowledge yielded by the humanities. On the single sense approach, for instance, one is apt to find the view that the study of the humanities yields systematic knowledge of what texts mean — what Blake's poems mean, what the Book of Job means, what Atwood's novel *The Edible Woman* means, and so on. The epistemology one would normally find associated with a single sense approach would be one that would stress the cumulative and more accurate knowledge of the meaning of texts. On the other hand, on the multiple sense approach, one is apt to find the view that the sort of knowledge one derives from the study of the humanities is self-knowledge, a greater awareness of one's self, one's potential, as a result of having been drawn outside oneself into the world of the text, a world which discloses itself in many different ways to participants who enter therein. This, in turn, represents quite a different epistemology.

There have been a variety of approaches for resolving this problem. I shall examine, first of all, two simplistic approaches and then move on to some more elaborate views. One extreme, simplistic and inadequate view is "extreme objectivism." This is the view that the meaning of the text is just what the text says. According to this position, the interpreter is instructed just to look at, or read, the text carefully and it will tell him what it means. The text, the object before the interpreter, is regarded as speaking directly to him. This characterization of interpretation represents an extreme single sense stance. This view is clearly inadequate. For one thing, texts as they stand are mute objects. They do not tell or say anything. On the contrary, texts must be made to speak. The interpreter must make them come alive. He must activate them, for without him, texts are silent. And, in so doing, in making texts speak, he cannot by-pass interpreting them, puzzling their sense out of the fabric of words and sentences and paragraphs. When he does this, we find, as I have already mentioned, that different activators of the text find different meanings in the text. Texts, it seems, do not speak with one voice.

While inadequate, this position yet contains some grains of truth. For one thing, the meaning of a text must somehow be found in, related to, and even justified by, the text. For another thing, even though he is the activator of its

## Interpretation: The One and the Many

saying anything, the interpreter should listen to the text, to hear what it has to say rather than what he would like it to say, or wished it had said.

Another extreme, inadequate and equally simplistic view is "extreme subjectivism," the view that because everyone is different, everyone is going to find a different meaning in the text. On this view, the interpreter will find his own personal meaning in the text, what the text means to him. This represents an extreme multiple sense approach, for it authorizes the widest range of interpretations possible. Sometimes this view simply represents the counsel of interpretive frustration. The interpreter finds too many interpretations with which to cope, and so, he asks, why bother sorting them all out? Why bother critically evaluating them? Some, for example, say that the Bible can be made to say anything. Therefore interpret it as you wish and each view, no matter how conflicting or how contradictory, is perfectly fine, for that person. This is an "all have won and all shall have prizes" interpretive approach.

Like extreme objectivism, extreme subjectivism is too simplistic and inadequate. For one thing, it does not acknowledge the legitimacy of the text as a coequal if not predominant partner in interpretation. It sets up the text to be raped by the interpreter, to be used simply for his own interpretive purposes, rather than lovingly coaxed or seduced into yielding up its meaning. For another thing, it ignores the extent to which understanding and communication in language are possible. While people do differ, there is sufficient overlap that through language people can converse, make themselves understood, and so share meaning.

This approach ignores the communality of meaning. While inadequate, there is yet a grain of truth in this approach as well. The interpreter, as well as the text, shares in the releasing of textual meaning. The interpreter's attitude, the extent to which he is willing to listen to the text, the whole text and not just selected snippets of it, is important. Moreover, the interpreter's perspective (his beliefs, commitments, his "horizon") plays a role in singling out what he considers important in the text. Finally, the interpreter's purposes in interpreting the text, whether a quick once-over or a more sustained look, are also significant in determining the extent to which the interpreter will search for meaning.

What should be learned from these two inadequate simplistic views is that textual interpretation takes place within a "dialectical tension," that is, that interpretation occurs within a movement back and forth between text, interpreter, text, interpreter, and so on, as the interpreter struggles to become clear about its meaning. The interpreter, on first reading, hazards a guess as to its meaning; then goes back to the text to see if this guess is borne out by the text itself, and, in so doing, notices other aspects of the text he initially missed; he revises his view in the light of this deeper awareness. This dialectical tension in interpretation is a familiar experience to all who have read a text more than once.

Another way of saying this is to say that in interpretation the interpreter enters into a "downward interpretive spiral vortex." Interpretation is a spiral movement between text, interpreter, text, interpreter, and so on, as the interpreter explores the world of the text, moving beyond superficial understanding (at the top of the spiral) to deeper levels of understanding (on the turns beneath). The image of a spiral vortex is a suggestive one. It suggests that one becomes drawn into a text. It suggests, moreover, that there are depths to a text to be explored. One becomes charmed or enchanted by the text, the further one explores it. One becomes aware of the world of the text, a world that may be quite different from the interpreter's own world. One becomes attuned to it. By entering ever more deeply into the world of the text one experiences the exhilaration of the humanities.

With this dialectical tension or downward interpretive spiral vortex in mind, let us examine more sophisticated versions of the single and multiple sense approaches. The view that texts should be regarded as having one and only one correct interpretation is, for the most part, a surprisingly modern view. While there were precursors,[3] it is a view that comes explicitly to the fore at the time of the Protestant Reformation. It was important, the Reformers maintained, that accurate knowledge of what the Bible says be obtained. This is important not for the aesthetic satisfaction of having mastered a text but rather because it concerned eternal salvation. Interpretation was a serious matter: one's entire eternal future could hang upon it.

The Protestant Reformers accomplished a whole reorientation in textual interpretation, away from the diversity of the allegorical tradition that preceded them. Very briefly, three significant aspects of this reorientation may be mentioned. First of all, they advocated a turning to the text, an obedient willingness to hear what it has to say. This involved in principle a turning away from the voice of tradition, church teaching, councils and creeds back to the primary texts of the religion, the writings of the Old and New Testaments. In advocating this they were advocating a single sense approach. An early Protestant Reformer, William Tyndale, put the matter this way: "Though shalt understand, therefore, that the scripture hath but one sense, which is the literal sense. And that literal sense is the root and ground of all, and the anchor that never faileth, whereunto if thou cleave, though canst never err or go out of the way."

In a similar vein, Calvin wrote: "Scripture, they say, is fertile and thus produces a variety of meanings. I acknowledge that Scripture is a most rich and inexhaustible fountain of all wisdom; but I deny that its fertility consists in the various meanings which any man, at his pleasure, may assign. Let us know, then, that the true meaning of Scripture is the natural and obvious meaning; and let us embrace and abide by it resolutely." Finding the literal, natural and obvious meaning of Scripture was to prove to be, however, a highly intricate matter, for the reorientation involved two further important shifts.

The new reorientation involved, secondly, a turning towards language. In the case of the Bible, this meant knowing Hebrew and Aramaic for the Old Testament; Greek, for the New. These languages had to be learned in order to grasp the meaning of key expressions in their original languages and to compensate for the loss of meaning that occurs in translation. It had, moreover, the effect of turning attention to the medium in which texts occur, namely, written language. Finally, the reorientation involved a turning towards history, to the historical circumstances surrounding the text and the events they report and interpret. Linked closely with a turning towards the text and its original language, the shift towards history essentially involved a focus on the original context of the text in an attempt to establish as accurately as possible, the meaning of the text within its original milieu. That one original meaning, that meaning-for-them-there-then, was the meaning the interpreter of the text should seek to ascertain.

The approach of the Protestant Reformers was profoundly influential on many branches of study in the following centuries, and, in turn, provoked many important meta-interpretive considerations concerning what constituted listening to a text and paying attention to language and history. In time the original Reformation approach itself underwent a profound reevaluation in the light of reflections by Schleiermacher, Hegel, Dilthey, Heidegger, and many others, on the nature of language and history.[4]

In *Validity in Interpretation*, E.D. Hirsch Jr. offers a spirited and stalwart defense of the view that texts should be regarded as having one right meaning.[5] Hirsch, a contemporary American literary theorist, points out that in literary criticism today there is a longstanding tradition of a rather easy going aesthetic appreciation of texts. He draws our attention to the sorts of words characteristically used to describe interpretations of texts, words such as "sensitive" or "plausible" (or similar words such as "rich," "insightful," "fruitful," "suggestive," "helpful," "illuminating"). Such adjectives, however,

## Interpretation: The One and the Many

serve to legitimize a rather congenial, non-judgmental and non-rigorous approach to textual interpretation. Hirsch contends that this approach, while fashionable, is far too lax. It sets up a rather cavalier attitude towards the text by the interpreter: he may take out of the text all sorts of views that are "sensitive" or "plausible" that may have very little to do with what the text actually means. After all, even interpretations which misunderstood the text can be said to be "sensitive" or "plausible." What is missing, Hirsch suggests, is an emphasis on accuracy of interpretation, on faithfulness to the original. The appropriate adjectives which should apply to interpretations are words like "valid" or "correct," adjectives which imply norms or criteria for judging interpretations. Not all interpretations of a text are of equal worth.

Some of the main claims that Hirsch makes about textual interpretation may be summarized as follows:

(a) A text has one and only one correct meaning.

A text is an act of communication between an author and reader. If the reader does not grasp what the author wishes to convey through writing that text, then the reader has understood neither the text nor the author. Authors write texts to convey something to their prospective readers and it is this meaning, Hirsch contends, that the interpreter should grasp.

(b) The one and only one correct meaning of a text is the author's intended meaning.

The alternative to this, Hirsch points out, is interpretive anarchy: "For if the meaning of a text is not the author's, then no interpretation can possibly correspond to the meaning of the text, since the text can have no determinate or determinable meaning." In defence of (b) Hirsch engages in Chapter One of *Validity in Interpretation* in a lively attack on the alternate view which he calls "semantic autonomy," the view that interpretation of texts may proceed independently of a consideration of the author's intended meaning.[6]

The implications of (a) and (b) are clear for textual interpretation:

> (c) The author's intended meaning is what the interpreter of the text should seek, for it represents the correct ("valid") meaning of the text.

How one goes about establishing the author's intended meaning is, of course, a complex story and in Chapter Five Hirsch offers some interesting suggestions.

This approach has raised a number of important questions. For one thing, Hirsch has vastly overstated his point.[7] It is often the case that knowing something about an author is *helpful*: when and where he lived; his language; his culture; his concerns; his other works; his objectives, as stated in a preface or introduction; the tradition in which he stands, and so on. Surely these are helpful in interpreting a text. But this is not to say that the author's intended meaning is the meaning of the text. Moreover, how does Hirsch's approach relate to texts whose authorship is in doubt — Plato's *Epinomis*, for instance, or "St. Paul's" Letter to the Ephesians? In addition, what about texts whose authorship is unknown, for example, most of the great epics, creation stories and sagas of most cultures, and even the Book of Job?

Finally, surely the best source of information about what an author intends is the text itself: that, after all, is what the author wrote. It is what the author has put forth on the public stage. There are, then, serious critical questions about the sort of single sense approach advocated by Hirsch and it is by no means clear how his position can be adapted to accommodate these concerns. Nor is it at all clear that the only alternative to Hirsch's position is a view of textual interpretation which would license interpretive arbitrariness. Hirsch may be right that some limits need to be imposed on what correctly constitutes an interpretation of a text. The key issues may be, however, what sort of limits are appropriate and the extent to which they can circumscribe one and only one meaning as the correct interpretation of the text.

Let us turn now to the multiple sense approach to the matter. This sort of approach is an ancient one, unlike the single sense view. The multiple sense approach grew fundamentally out of the problems concerning how to interpret sacred texts in a modern sophisticated age while somehow still preserving the sacred quality of those texts. For ancient Greek thinkers who developed this view the problem was how to interpret the rather subhuman activities and pronouncements of the gods in Hesiod and Homer. For ancient Jewish and Christian thinkers the problem was how to make sense of the crudities involved in biblical works while not demeaning the character of the God about whom the Bible speaks. The solution was a theory of multiple senses: different kinds, or levels, of interpretation. A story, gross on its literal superficial meaning, was held to have a different, much more profound, interpretation when viewed allegorically.

I want to mention briefly two multiple sense approaches, one ancient and one modern. The ancient view goes back to Origen, an early Christian theologian and philosopher, who (along with modifications by John Cassian and Saint Augustine) put forward a position that launched a twelve-hundred year tradition in textual interpretation. In *On First Principles* Origen claims that texts have three types of senses.

There is, first of all, a superficial understanding which consists of the literal, historical meaning of the text. Thus, in accordance with this sort of interpretation, an interpreter might view the story of the Exodus in Exodus 1-15:21 simply in terms of Moses leading his people out of Egypt under Yahweh's guidance during the reign of Ramesis II or the Parable of the Good Samaritan in Luke 10:29-37 as an example of a mugging on the Jerusalem-to-Jericho road which fortunately had a happy outcome.

There is, secondly, a more advanced sort of interpretation which consists of the moral meaning of the text. In accordance with this type of interpretation, an interpreter might see in the story of the Exodus an example of dedicated leadership, or regard the Parable of the Good Samaritan as an example of how to behave towards strangers in need of help.

Finally, Origen suggests, there is a much more advanced means of interpretation which consists of the allegorical meaning of the text. In keeping with this kind of interpretation, an interpreter might discern in the story of Moses' liberation of his people a foreshadowing of Jesus' liberation of people from sin. Similarly, on this level, an interpreter might come to see that in the Parable of the Good Samaritan the mugging is much more than a simple physical beating but represents a profound statement of the utter helplessness of the human condition beset by sin and that the Samaritan is a disclosure of the true identity of the one who truly helps and heals.

For Origen the approach had many merits. For one thing, it overcame crude conceptions of God in passages where he is depicted as engaged in human activities (such as walking and talking), changing his mind, and urging vengeance in a manner unbecoming to deity. It allowed, moreover, for growth in understanding as the reader entered much more fully into the life of the text. In addition, it incorporated the reader into active participation in the text's meaning, inviting, coaxing, even demanding him to think creatively and imaginatively about the text's meaning. Moreover, it was for Origen an approach that was specifically authorized by the text in question.

Origen's tripartite division of the sorts of senses was expanded by Cassian and Augustine into a fourfold model. This framework for interpretation became the standard one for understanding texts until the Protestant Reformation.[8] From a quite different perspective, a more recent multiple sense approach has been proposed by the contemporary hermeneutic philosopher, Hans-Georg Gadamer. In a monumental work, *Truth and Method*, Gadamer develops a new understanding of the humanities and textual interpretation.[9] Just a few themes from this work relevant to the topic before us will be singled out for mention.

The single sense approach to textual interpretation rests on an assumption, namely, that the humanities represent a body of knowledge, having a methodology and yielding results comparable to but distinct from the natural sciences. Gadamer traces Dilthey's continually thwarted attempt to work out "a critique of historical reason," Dilthey's ambitious project to develop a comprehensive account of the epistemology of the humanities that would simultaneously do justice to the historical nature of such inquiries and yet produce reliable knowledge that would be on a par with that yielded by scientific method. The project, Gadamer points out, was set within the parameters of the assumption that the humanities, like the sciences, possess an epistemology and a methodology. It is this fundamental assumption that Gadamer calls into question.

According to Gadamer, Dilthey's failure was instructive: it finally exposed the folly of the Cartesian assumption that the cognitive structure of the humanities is akin to, although different from, that of the sciences. As Gadamer says, "the conflict that he [Dilthey] tried to resolve shows clearly what pressure the methodology of modern science exerts and what our task must be: namely, to describe more adequately the experience of the human sciences and the objectivity they are able to achieve."[10] If this assumption is to be rejected, then how should the humanities be understood? Gadamer proceeds to develop "the foundations of a theory of hermeneutical experience," drawing chiefly on the contributions of Heidegger who shifted the notion of understanding away from considerations of methodology to a characteristic of the being of human life itself. In so doing he introduces three key terms: "prejudice," "fusion of horizons" and "application."

All interpretation proceeds by way of "prejudice," the interpreter's own positioning of himself before the text in such a way that the self is not eradicated, nor viewed as eradicated. The point is important, for it involves the denial of all views that would regard the interpreter as a diaphanous, dispassionate transmitter of meaning. The interpreter is not that sort of being: rather, he is one with beliefs, interests, prejudgments, expectations, and (of special interest to Gadamer) is one who stands within tradition. These aspects of the interpreter cannot be denied: "we stand always within tradition, and this is no objectifying process, i.e., we do not conceive of what tradition says as something other, something alien." He adds: "All that is asked is that we remain open to the meaning of the other person or of the text. But this openness always includes our placing the other meaning in a relation with the whole of our own meanings or ourselves in relation to it." Just as "prejudice" points to a robustness of self which cannot be denied, so too, Gadamer's notion of the "fusion of horizons" points to a mutual resilience of both text and interpreter. It is not as if one must succumb to the other, to make the past present, or the present past, thereby eradicating one of the partners in the interpretive transaction. For Gadamer, the matter is much more complex:

> this means that the interpreter's own thoughts have also gone into the re-awakening of the meaning of the text. In this the interpreter's own horizon is decisive, yet not as a personal standpoint that one holds on to or enforces, but more as a meaning and a possibility that one brings into play and puts at risk, and that helps one truly to make one's own what is said in the text. I have described this above as a "fusion of horizons." We can now see that this is the full realisation of conversation, in which something is expressed that is not only mine or my author's, but common.[11]

Finally, there is application, a much neglected aspect of hermeneutics, Gadamer observes (although it should be noted that Origen clearly recognized its worth). Both religious and legal texts, Gadamer contends, make a claim on the interpreter: to be understood, they must be applied, either in connection with salvation (religious texts) or justice (legal texts). This is a rather strong claim. It is not as if understanding a text is one thing and then application an optional extra. As Gadamer portrays the situation, application "essentially and necessarily" belongs to understanding. He appeals to the example of understanding an order: "To understand the order means to apply it to the specific situation to which it is relevant." He applies this to all texts in the humanities: understanding necessarily involves application.

Gadamer's approach, like Hirsch's, raises some critical questions. For one thing, how is it possible both to acknowledge the unavoidable role of "prejudices" and yet be open to the text's meaning? How, moreover, is a "fusion of horizons" to be achieved? And, finally, is Gadamer correct in maintaining that understanding necessarily involves application? Cannot one be said to understand a text without thereby necessarily relating its meaning either to one's self or one's situation?

However these problems be resolved, Gadamer's approach to the humanities has some clear implications for the meta-interpretive problem of the one and the many. One important consequence of his notion of application is the following: "all reading involves application, so that a person reading a text is himself part of the meaning he apprehends. He belongs to the text that he is reading....He can, indeed he must, accept the fact that future generations will understand differently what he has read in the text." More generally, Gadamer puts the matter this way: "The text is to be made to speak through interpretation. But no text and no book speaks if it does not speak the language that reaches the other person. Thus interpretation must find the right language if it really wants to make the text speak. There cannot, therefore, be any one interpretation that is correct 'in itself,' precisely because every interpretation is concerned with the text itself....Every interpretation has to adapt itself to the hermeneutical situation to which it belongs."

As is now evident, probing the problem of the one and the many opens up many complex issues. These questions, however, are mere surface manifestations of a much deeper level of controversy, one that has fundamentally to do with the assumptions made about the nature of textual interpretation. Gadamer has already exposed one such presupposition — the one that beset Dilthey's project. There are others.

For one thing, what is it that interpreting a text yields? What is an interpreted meaning? It might be viewed, for instance, as the beholding of a transparent meaning enshrined in a text, an interpretive adoration of the meaning of the text in all its untouched splendor. Or it might be viewed simply as the release of the meaning pent up by the text. On either of these views, the presupposition is that interpretation is to be regarded as the comprehension of an "it," a text-embedded meaning as it is in-itself. The interpreter, then, is the instrument by means of which "it" comes to light. The interpreted meaning is the "it" which has been placed in the text and which awaits unveiling. It is a view of interpreted meaning which is congruent with a single sense approach, for the "it" would represent the one and only one correct meaning the interpreter should ascertain.

On the other hand, a very different picture of interpretation is obtained if one follows the suggestion that interpretive experience discloses understanding as involving a dialectical tension or as representing an entanglement in a spiral vortex as an interpreter comes to know a work better, asking it questions and imaginatively having it put questions to him. The imagery here of a tension or a vortex is a suggestive one, for it leads one to recognize that there is no finality to interpretation, no exhaustion of all meaning, for the process can always continue. This also necessitates the recognition that in interpretation there is no assuredness on the part of the interpreter that he has found "it." (Indeed, on this view, it might be contended that there is no "it" there to be grasped.) Interpretation, on this view, involves risk, a tentative putting forth on the part of the interpreter a claim concerning what a text "might mean" or "could mean," never what it "must mean." Interpreted meaning then becomes a meaning created at least in part by the interpreter's effort and skills. It is a presupposition that would accord well with a multiple sense approach, for, on this view of interpreted meaning, it would not be surprising but very likely that the one and same text will be interpreted differently by different interpreters.

There is, moreover, a further conflict concerning the role of the interpreter. On the one hand, there is what might be called a "subordinationist" position that claims that the text is paramount and that the interpreter must be subordinate to it. This view calls for the interpreter to cloak or mask or "bracket" his stance so as to uncover "its" meaning, an epistemology or ontology of dubious merit in the post-Heideggerian period. It is, however, a view that is congruent with a single sense approach, for it sets forth a presupposition about the nature of interpretation that must be true if the interpreter is accurately and faithfully to capture "it." On the other hand, there is what might be dubbed an "interactionist" view of the interpreter's role, one which regards him as a coequal partner in the creation of the text's meaning. This position does not, of course, deny the importance of the text in the interpretive transaction: it simply acknowledges its status as coequal. In many ways this presupposition fits the multiple sense views of Origen, who stresses the interpreter's level of comprehension, and Gadamer, who emphasizes the fusion of horizons in the determination of the text's meaning.

This dispute over the interpreter's role is closely associated with one further conflict, one having to do with different conceptions of the nature of texts in the humanities. Are such works to be regarded as instruments for the transmission of messages? Such a view would postulate a one-way movement of meaning, from text to interpreter, hopefully with as little disturbance as possible in the process. Such a view would appear to be a presupposition of single sense approaches to textual interpretation, and it would furthermore imply a subordinationist model of the interpreter's role. It is a view which runs into considerable difficulties in the light of interpretive experience and the post-Heideggerian conception of the person of the interpreter. On the other hand, should works in the humanities be regarded more as occasions for the sharing in meaning? Such a view would postulate a two-way movement of meaning, as something which occurs between text and interpreter in the creation or determination of a shared meaning. This latter view fits the presupposition of the interpreter's role as a coequal interactionist.

Everywhere, Dilthey said, understanding opens up a world. By entering into a text through interpretation, the interpreter enters a world he cannot otherwise enter, for the humanities have a distinctive autonomous region. The interpreter becomes a different person, aware of different stances, different possibilities, and different ways of looking at things. He has changed, for his horizon has been extended. The interpreter, then, is like the Connecticut Yankee who enters the world of King Arthur's court. He cannot stay there nor can he ever be an integral part of that court. But, on returning, he is different, for he is a Connecticut Yankee who has been at King Arthur's court. That is a rare accomplishment. He has in a sense, as Eliot pointed out, arrived where he started and now knows that place for the first time.

This paper began with quotations from T.S. Eliot and Wilhelm Dilthey and a question concerning how these are to be interpreted. Perhaps in the light of the ensuing discussion concerning single sense and multiple sense approaches, and especially in the light of the fundamentally divergent presuppositions concerning interpreted meaning, the role of the interpreter, and the nature of texts in the humanities, it might be better to ask, what is interpretation?

## ENDNOTES

[1] For a critical discussion of six modern definitions of hermeneutics, see Richard E. Palmer, *Hermeneutics* (Evanston: Northwestern University Press, 1969), chapter 3.

[2] See, for example, the many different interpretations of Shakespeare's *Hamlet* discussed by Morris Weitz in *Hamlet and the Philosophy of Literary Criticism* (London: Faber & Faber, 1965) or by Paul Gottschalk in *The Meanings of Hamlet* (Albuquerque: University of New Mexico Press, 1972). Similarly, Norman Perrin in *Jesus and the Language of the Kingdom* (Philadelphia: Fortress Press, 1976), chapter 3, surveys and discusses a wide range of recent interpretive approaches to the parables of Jesus.

[3] The Antiochene School of exegesis is often cited in this regard. For a fuller discussion, see Robert M. Grant, "History of the Interpretation of the Bible, I," in *The Interpreter's Bible*, I (New York: Abingdon Press, 1952), pp. 106-114 and James D. Wood, *The Interpretation of the Bible* (London: Duckworth, 1958), chapter 5. Unfortunately, however, many of the key statements of the Antiochene position, including Theodore of Mopsuestia's "On Allegory and History" and Diodorus of Tarsus' "What is the Difference between Theory and Allegory?" are no longer extant.

[4] For a brief introduction to this reevaluation within Protestant hermeneutics, see Ernst Fuchs, "The New Testament and the Hermeneutical Problem," in James D. Robinson and John B. Cobb, Jr. (eds.), *The New Hermeneutic* (New York: Harper & Row, 1964).

[5] *Validity in Interpretation* (New Haven: Yale Univ. Press, 1967).

[6] Those who advance such a position include, according to Hirsh, Eliot and Pound and their followers (including Wellek and Warren), Heidegger and his followers (including Bultmann and Gadamer), and Jung and his disciples.

[7] For critical discussions of Hirsch's hermeneutical position, see especially the following: Palmer, pp. 60-65; Quentin Skinner, "Motives, Intentions and the Interpretation of Texts," *New Literary History* 3 (1972), 393-408; John Reichert, *Making Sense of Literature* (Chicago: Univ. of Chicago Press, 1977), chapter 4; and Barrie A. Wilson, "Hirsch's Hermeneutics: A Critical Examination," *Philosophy Today* 22 (1978), 20-33 [reprinted in this volume]. For Hirsch's

continued defense of his approach, see the essays contained in his later work, *The Aims of Interpretation* (Chicago: University of Chicago Press, 1976).

[8]The influence of this interpretive schema, and its many modifications, has been traced in Beryl Smalley, *The Study of the Bible in the Middle Ages* (Notre Dame: University of Notre Dame Press, 1964).

[9]Hans-Georg Gadamer, *Truth and Method* (New York: Seabury Press, 1975). Originally published as *Wahreit und Methode* (1960).

[10]*Ibid.*, p. 214.

[11]*Ibid.*, p. 350.

# PART TWO:

# HERMENEUTIC CRITIQUES

# CHAPTER 2

# DILTHEY'S DILEMMA

## 1. Introduction

Throughout his philosophical writings Dilthey strove to provide solid epistemological and methodological foundations for the *Geisteswissenschaften*.[1] His contributions to hermeneutics arose out of these investigations into the theoretical foundations of the humanities. Indeed, in Dilthey's thought, hermeneutics became a theory of the humanities.

In this article I will reconstruct and examine a line of argument that paves the way for an important dilemma with which hermeneutics and the theory of the humanities must eventually grapple.[2] This dilemma concerns how it is possible to reconcile in one hermeneutic theory (or in one theory of the humanities) the demands of both *Verstehen* and *Allgemeingültigkeit* (objective validity).[3]

Dilthey's argument is reconstructed from a variety of writings,[4] notably from *Die Einleitung in die Geisteswissenschaften*,[5] *Die Entstehung der Hermeneutik*,[6] *Entwürfe zur Kritik der Historischen Vernunft*,[7] and *Der Aufbau der Geschichtlichen Welt in den Geisteswissenschaften*.[8] While none of these works sets forth Dilthey's line of reasoning exactly as it is presented here, it is intended that the reconstruction faithfully represent an important strand in Dilthey's thought, one that leads to a dilemma for hermeneutics and constitutes in Dilthey's judgment the central problem for the theory of the humanities. The dilemma also serves to indicate the framework within which subsequent theories of textual interpretation have occurred.

## 2. The Humanities and the Natural Sciences

According to Dilthey there is an important distinction between the humanities and the natural sciences. In Dilthey's estimation, both now lack secure theoretical foundations. Of special interest to him, however, is the problematic nature of the humanities. What is problematic about the humanities? Why are they problematic? How has this situation come about? And how are the humanities to be distinguished from the natural sciences? In order to answer these questions, and in order to see furthermore why the task of providing epistemological and methodological foundations for the humanities was regarded by Dilthey as so urgent, it is first necessary to consider the context in which he raises these questions.

In the *Vorrede* to the *Autobiographisches*,[9] Dilthey characterizes the philosophical situation in his youth as having been one in which the unifying philosophy of Hegel had loosened its hold on the natural sciences. Simultaneously, Dilthey points out, scientists were attempting to treat human values and human reality "as a product of Nature."[10] He further reflects:

> It was out of this situation that the predominant impulse in my philosophical thought arose, the desire to understand (*verstehen*) life in its own terms. I had the desire to press even deeper into the world of the historical (*die geschichtliche Welt*),[11] to become aware of its soul; and the philosophical effort to find a way into these realities, to establish their validity (*Gültigkeit*), and to ensure objective knowledge (*objektive Erkenntnis*) of them — this urge was for me only the other side of my desire to probe even deeper in the world of the historical.[12]

The breakup of knowledge into the humanities on the one side and the natural sciences on the other, the widening distance between History or Spirit on the one hand and Nature on the other, was symptomatic, Dilthey thought, of the dissolution of what he termed *"die europäische Metaphysik"* (the European Metaphysical System).[13] This system of thought was not a particular metaphysical system but represented, Dilthey claimed, the underlying views of various metaphysical outlooks propounded by European philosophers over many centuries. It had served to integrate man's understanding of himself socially, religiously, and intellectually – and not just the philosophers' understanding of man but the view of man shared by most Europeans: "the western farmer in America" or "the fisherman off the coasts of Sicily or Iceland."[14] The European Metaphysical System rested on three basic motifs:

(1) the notion of a universal order intelligible to man

(2) the value placed on people as volitional agents whose history is of importance, and

(3) a belief in divine salvation.[15]

This synthesis, fashioned out of Greek, Roman, and Judaeo-Christian traditions, held together the varied activities of man and endowed them with worthwhileness. It continued "so long as the situation of science remained unchanged."[16]

The rise of *die europäische Metaphysik* Dilthey traces in the Second Book of *Die Einleitung in die Geisteswissenschaften* and in a variety of studies included in volume II of his *Gesammelte Schriften*.[17] The collapse of this worldview is treated in a preliminary fashion at the end of the Second Book of *Die Einleitung* in a section entitled *"Die Auflösung der metaphysischen Stellung des Menschen zur Wirklichkeit."*[18] Here he promised a further work on the history of modern epistemologically oriented scientific awareness in relation to the study of man himself. Dilthey never wrote this work, but a series of articles can be viewed as sections of such a work.[19]

From this series of works Friess reconstructs Dilthey's argument showing the phases in the demise of *die europäische Metaphysik* and the current state of the humanities. It provides the background out of which Dilthey's dilemma arises. Friess' reconstruction of the stages Dilthey identifies in the dissolution of the European Metaphysical System is as follows. First of all, Friess notes, Dilthey indicates that "the natural sciences, which in the early modern period gained a new footing in concepts independent of the traditional metaphysics of substantial forms, are not metaphysically oriented."[20] This raises serious questions concerning the theoretical foundations of the natural sciences. They have arisen out of the metaphysical matrix of the classical world view, yet at the same time, they have not only severed connections with their foundations but also called into question the tenability of those foundations themselves.

Even new attempts to ground the methodology of the natural sciences have failed. Dilthey mentions that Descartes had thought that,

> If one presents these presuppositions [the presuppositions of the mathematical natural sciences] in clear concepts and propositions, and understands why they are objectively valid, a constructive method can be built upon them. In this way the mechanistic view first won its certainty and showed the possibility of further extension.[21]

The "constructive method" failed; however, as Dilthey points out, it "succumbed to the critique of knowledge by Locke, Hume, and Kant."[22] Not only are the natural sciences metaphysically adrift; they cannot become another European Metaphysical System with the same scope and force in men's lives as the former one possessed, for the natural sciences explain only one sort of experience (and not all of experience), and they claim no finality to their concepts (as did the European Metaphysical System).

Secondly, Friess notes, Dilthey indicates that "coincident with new orientation of natural sciences, fresh viewpoints with regard to human nature appeared, and the attempt was made to develop a natural knowledge of man's world, a natural theology, religion, law, *etc.*"[23] That is, one response to the breakup of the European Metaphysical System consisted of the attempt to view all of human experience from the vantage point of the methodology of the natural sciences. Dilthey describes this attempt in *The Essence of Philosophy* as follows:

> David Hume in his *Treatise of Human Nature* saw in the empirical study of man the true philosophy. As he repudiated metaphysics, based epistemology exclusively on the new psychology, and in this psychology also showed the explanatory principles for the human studies, an introspectively grounded system of these studies arose...John Stuart Mill, like Hume, wanted philosophy to mean "the scientific knowledge of man as an intellectual, moral, and social being."[24]

Dilthey refers to this attempt to scientize all human knowledge as *"das natürliche System der Geisteswissenschaften"*[25] — again to regard Spirit as a product of Nature, as the Encyclopaedists, Comte, and the more philosophically oriented scientists of Germany tried to do.[26] Dilthey acknowledges that the contributions of Hume, Mill, and Comte to the study of the humanities were very great indeed. But basically this heroic positivistic attempt mutilated human experience: "its limitation was that it maimed the spiritual world (*die geistige Welt*) to fit the scope of the outer world."[27]

The *natürliche* approach to the humanities had two major consequences. First of all, it "proved unable to do justice to the fullness of the historical world in thought and political action."[28] Dilthey claims that the methodology of the natural sciences is inappropriate for the exploration of human reality with which the humanities are properly concerned. Secondly, this approach not only failed to grasp human experience, thereby distorting the humanities, but also demonstrated an important feature of the natural sciences themselves. The disastrous results obtained by the imposition of this approach upon the humanities indicated that not only were the natural sciences separated from their original metaphysical moorings but they were also cut off from any connection with human experience:

> Natural sciences lift out of lived experience (*Erlebnis*) only partial contents which can help to determine changes in the physical world, independent of us. So knowledge of nature deals merely with appearances for consciousness. The subject-matter of the human studies, on the other hand, is the inwardly-given reality of the lived experiences themselves.[29]

That domain of experience which the methodology of the natural sciences cannot probe Dilthey often calls "*Erlebnis*." According to Hodges, "*Das Erleben* is the mode in which we experience our own states or psychical acts in the actual having of them, and it differs from all other modes in which we can be conscious of ourselves in that it is an immediate experience."[30] The failure of the *natürliche* approach to the humanities only succeeded in magnifying the gap between Nature and Spirit or History.

A reaction to the positivistic approach set in and a third stage in the dissolution of the European Metaphysical System arose. In Friess' reconstruction, this third phase rejected the *natürliche* approach. Dilthey cites the important contributions of philosophers such as Schelling, Schleiermacher, Hegel, and Schopenhauer who posited the systematic unity of consciousness and set out to do justice to the humanities. For Dilthey this represented the most ambitious attempt of the human mind to find a philosophical method which differed from the procedures of the natural sciences on which metaphysics could be based. Some in this undertaking reached back to Kant and Fichte, others to Leibniz. But the attempt floundered and finally failed. In Dilthey's judgment,

> They heaped up hypotheses, which in the inaccessible realm beyond experience found no firm ground, but also no resistance. Here one set of hypotheses was just as plausible as another. How could this metaphysics have fulfilled the mission of giving certainty and security to individual and social life in the great crises of the century!...Even this metaphysical method does not find the bridge, leading from necessity as a fact of our consciousness to objective validity (*objektiven Geltung*). And in vain it seeks a way from the systematic unity of consciousness to the insight that this unity is the inner bond of reality itself.[31]

Moreover, Dilthey observes, "over the system of their ideas fell the shadows of the twilight of metaphysics."[32] The European Metaphysical System has collapsed, and neither the natural scientific nor the unity of consciousness approach has replaced it.

The situation Dilthey finds for the humanities is this. The sciences, divorced from their original metaphysical roots, have tried to account for all of experience, even experience which is distinctively human. In this they have failed, for, Dilthey maintains, there is a domain of experience which eludes the approach of the natural sciences and which is, moreover, of immense importance for human comprehension. This represents a crucial step in

Dilthey's argument; it constitutes his critique of empiricism; and in his own estimation it establishes a basis upon which the humanities can be erected.[33] Various of Dilthey's concepts — Life (*das Leben*), lived experience (*Erlebnis, das Erleben*), the spiritual world (*die Geistige Welt*), the world of the historical (*die geschichtliche Welt*) — point to a domain of experience which is inaccessible from the point of view of natural scientific methodology.

The *natürliche* system of the humanities is not and cannot be an authentic account of the humanities. Yet the humanities, which did make sense within the European Metaphysical System, can no longer be made sense of within that integrating worldview. And no subsequent system, whether originating in positivism or in German Idealism, has emerged to replace that system. Indeed, in Dilthey's view, no such approach can replace the classical world outlook. If it is true, as Dilthey claims, that there exists a domain of experience which natural science cannot comprehend, and if the European Metaphysical System has collapsed without replacement, then the question arises how such a domain of experience with which the humanities is concerned can be discerned, explored, and grounded within a framework that does not simply revert to the classical worldview. This is the problem that Dilthey poses for the theory of the humanities.

The first step in Dilthey's argument which ultimately leads him to a dilemma is: (call this point 'D1')

> D1. There is an important distinction to be made between the humanities and the natural sciences.

Though distinct from the natural sciences, the humanities are nonetheless problematic, partly because they are no longer grounded within an all-encompassing view of experience and knowledge, and partly because the approach to the subject matter of the humanities has been seriously challenged by the positivistic point of view.

Because of claim D1 and also because, for Dilthey, there is a type of experience which differs from the sort of experience with which the natural sciences investigate, there is another important claim to be made:

> D2. Any attempt to develop a theory about the humanities must do justice to the sort of experience with which the humanities are properly concerned.

Exactly what constitutes this sort of experience, and how it is accessible, are matters which Dilthey struggled throughout his life to make clear. But there is a further claim. Not only are the humanities distinct from the natural sciences, they must be regarded at the very least as on a par with them, as being equal in cognitive worth. Two main reasons support this contention. First of all, the inner world of the humanities, lived experience, has to do with what is distinctively human. Furthermore, according to Dilthey the humanities must be regarded as having epistemological significance. If this were not the case, then the study of what is distinctively human would be regarded as of inferior worth to the study of the sciences.[34] Thus Dilthey claims:

> D3. Any attempt to develop a theory about the humanities must do justice to the cognitive worth of the humanities.

The two considerations expressed in D2 and D3 set requirements for what in Dilthey's estimation would constitute an adequate account of the nature of the humanities. They tend to lead Dilthey's thought in two quite different directions. The first consideration, namely doing justice to the sort of experience that typifies the humanities, leads Dilthey's thought in the direction of

*Verstehen.* The second consideration, doing justice to the epistemological claims of the humanities, leads him in the direction of *Allgemeingültigkeit*. They also give rise to the epistemological task that Dilthey called "*Kritik der historischen Vernunft*" or "*Grundlegung der Geisteswissen-schaften*,"[35] a project having to do with the conditions under which historical understanding, and therefore the humanities, is possible. Dilthey mentions this project in the *Entwürfe* as follows:

> The connections in the mind-affected world (*die geistige Welt*) arise in the human subject and it is the effort of the mind to determine the systematic meaning of that world which links the individual logical processes involved to each other. Thus, on the one hand, the comprehending subject creates this mind-affected world and, on the other, tries to gain objective knowledge of it. Hence we face the problem, how does the mental construction of the mind-affected world make knowledge of mind-affected reality possible? Earlier I have described this task as a critique of historical reason.[36]

The epistemological requirement for an accurate account of the humanities posed some extremely difficult problems for Dilthey: how is *knowledge* of *die geistige Welt* possible? As Friess points out,

> The progressive accumulation of knowledge in specific fields was at that time very impressive, and Dilthey, like Comte and Mill, wished to see the study of man and his culture pass from the control of theological and metaphysical speculation to a scientific basis.[37]

Dilthey rejected the positivistic approach but not its interests in epistemology: the hermeneutic task becomes, in his eyes, a way of finding a tool which opens up the realities of the humanities for inspection while also ensuring their validity. More will be said about this epistemological consideration in due course.

D1 claims *that* there is an important distinction to be drawn between the humanities and the natural sciences. In making this claim, by pointing to the factors which have led to the demise of the European Metaphysical System he has also made clear *why* they differ. What remains to be discussed is *how* they differ. This takes us in the direction required by D2.

In the *Aufbau* Dilthey notes that the *Geisteswissenschaften* include the following subject matters: "history; economics; law; political science; the study of religion, literature, and poetry; architecture; music; philosophical world views and systems; and finally psychology."[38] What unites this group of disciplines? Dilthey answers this question in several ways: they all have to do with *die geistige Welt*, this type of experience which natural scientific investigation cannot probe. They all "have reference to the same fact, humanity,"[39] or "in the humanities, a connection between Life and knowledge is retained so that thought arising from Life remains the foundation of intellectual creation."[40]

There is, however, another basis upon which Dilthey distinguishes the humanities and the natural sciences — *Das Verstehen*.

## 3. Das Verstehen

Dilthey makes a further claim:

> D4.D2 requires the recognition that the humanities employ a different mode of cognition than do the natural sciences.

The sort of experience on which the humanities rest is accessible only in and through *Verstehen*. It constitutes, for Dilthey, the only mode of inquiry appropriate to the humanities. As he points out,

> Understanding (*Verstehen*) and interpretation (*Deuten*) is the method which permeates the humanities. All functions are united in it. It contains all the truths of the humanities. At every point understanding opens up a world.[41]

*Verstehen* opens up to human comprehension the world of *Das Leben*. As such, it differs from "explanation" (*Erklärung*) which constitutes the natural scientific mode of cognition.[42] What, then, is *Verstehen*? How is it possible? And what does it make possible?

The distinction between explanation and understanding as modes of cognition was not a new one, although Dilthey's use of it, linking *Verstehen* to *Erlebnis* and thereby seeking to clarify the methodology of the humanities, was much more extensive. In outlining the nature of the historical method, Droysen had already made the distinction,[43] and had indicated the importance of the world of the historical for understanding in the humanities.[44] Even before Droysen, Schleiermacher had effected a turning point in hermeneutics,[45] by focusing attention on the role of understanding as such in textual interpretation. His contributions in this area heavily influenced Dilthey, especially two major emphases which "inaugurated a new beginning of understanding and its possibilities."[46]

At the outset of *Die kompendienartige Darstellung von 1819* Schleiermacher pointed out that hermeneutics exists only as a collection of specialized hermeneutics,[47] and urged that this fractionalization of interpretation — *i.e.*, understanding in this or in that particular field of study — be overcome and be replaced by an "*allgemeine Hermeneutik.*"[48] In this way Schleiermacher envisaged that hermeneutics would become the study of understanding in general, regardless of what is being understood.

This first emphasis in Schleiermacher's hermeneutic position represents a moving away from a preoccupation over the relationship of an interpreter with a literary monument, the text, towards the realization that in and through the text there is an author who seeks to communicate. The hermeneutic relationship changes from one of the interpreter to the text to that of the interpreter to the author of the text. This changed relationship necessitates a corresponding change in hermeneutics: from understanding the text to understanding another who speaks in and through the text.

For Schleiermacher the art of understanding texts becomes like the art of understanding someone else speaking in conversation. In such a situation the attention of the speakers is riveted not so much upon the words spoken *per se* as upon obtaining an understanding of what the other is saying by means of them.[49] The focus in hermeneutics is adjusted, then, from the plane of the words themselves to the plane of the understanding that exists, or ought to exist, between reader and author just as between one speaker and another. Interpreting becomes an enactment of the accord that should obtain between reader and author. Hermeneutics, as the theory of the art of understanding, becomes the investigation of understanding: what it is, and how it is possible.

The planes of language and of understanding between interpreter and author are not, however, disassociated. In *Hermeneutik Erster Entwurf* Schleiermacher observes that hermeneutics "develops out of two different points: understanding in language and understanding into the speaker."[50] And in *Die kompendienartige Darstellung von 1819* he further notes that:

> As in every speech there is a double relationship to both the totality of language and to the entire thought of its author, so, too, there exists in all understanding of the

speech two moments: understanding it as something produced out of language and understanding it as a fact (*Thatsache*) in the author's thinking.[51]

These two "moments" constitute a second major emphasis in Schleiermacher's hermeneutics. The first moment, understanding in language, involves grammatical interpretation. Whatever the text means, its meaning must be consistent with the possible meanings that the words and sentences have as syntactically arranged. But there is more to the moment of language than philology, for language itself points to the author's thought. Niebuhr points this out:

> Schleiermacher preferred to describe a word as a historical, dynamic entity whose precise meaning in any given occurrence can be determined only when we consider its relations to the entire development of the body of speech within which it lives. Even when the individuality of the speaker or writer is more significantly present in his discourse, his language constitutes an inheritance that qualifies his spirit, conditioning the direction and the progress of his thoughts.[52]

Language, then, conditions the author's thoughts: it sets limits to it. But there is a reciprocal action, for the language itself is chosen by the author himself in setting forth his thoughts, and in textual interpretation the interpreter must move beyond grammar to discern the author's choice of language, regarding the author as a volitional agent actively molding language to suit *his* thought.

This moment of interpretation, however, does not suffice for full understanding, for Schleiermacher's distinctive emphasis arose out of his views on history and human nature and the way in which humans understand one another. As Niebuhr says:

> Interpretation, Schleiermacher was convinced, does not belong to philology alone, because it has its origin in that nuclear life structure that transcends the vision of every particular science. It is rooted in the constitution of man as an ethical agent. The level of human nature from which it rises is accessible only to thinking that is informed by both empirical and constructive, theoretical interests in man....Speaking and interpreting presuppose participation in a common humanity but at the same time they give a new concreteness to that which is distinctively human in our experience of others and of ourselves.[53]

This second moment in interpretation, what Schleiermacher calls "technical" or "psychological" understanding, would have the interpreter examine what is individual about the text in question. This requires placing the work within the context of the author's life as a whole, coming to see his purpose, his encounters with experience, discerning even unconscious elements in his thought, and thereby understanding through "divination"[54] or reconstruction the thought of the author, This leads Schleiermacher to assert the maxim that an interpreter, by bringing into consciousness much of what remained unconscious for the author, could understand an author better than he understood himself.[55]

Dilthey adapted Schleiermacher's notion of understanding but broadened it so as to include not only the interpretation of texts but also all comprehension of human phenomena, and deepened it so as to include not just the empathic reconstruction of the author's thought but also the discernment of all human experience. Understanding becomes the way to Life.

For Dilthey, *Verstehen* is a method, and it is described in a variety of ways. In one place in *Der Aufbau* he writes:

> Life, experience of life, and the human studies are, thus, constantly related and interacting. It is not conceptual procedure which forms the foundation of the human studies but the becoming aware of a mental state in its totality and the rediscovering of it by empathy. Here life grasps life and the power with which these two basic procedures of the human studies are carried out preconditions their adequacy in all their branches.[56]

In this passage, understanding appears to be a psychological process, a means whereby one person enters imaginatively, empathically, or emotionally into the situation or outlook of another, recreating the other's experience in himself, and thereby understanding it. Dilthey often speaks in this way, as if understanding in the psychological sense is what he means by *Verstehen*. Dilthey, along with other defenders of *Verstehen* (*e.g.*, Collingwood and various social scientists cited by Abel), has been interpreted as claiming (a) that *Verstehen* represents a psychological, emphatic process, and (b) that *Verstehen* is a process which yields knowledge not otherwise obtainable about events.[57] Defenders of *Verstehen* such as Scriven[58] attempt to support (b) — as Scriven puts it, that "empathy is, in principle, a reliable tool for the historian and the physical scientist."[59] Critics of *Verstehen* such as Zilsel, Abel and Van Evra deny (b). Abel, for instance, finds that "the operation of *Verstehen* does not, however, add to our store of knowledge, because it consists of the application of knowledge already validated by personal experience; nor does it serve as a means of verification."[60]

> The understanding of other persons and life-expressions is built on our own experience, and on the continuous interplay of experience and understanding. But here we are concerned neither with logical construction nor

> psychological analysis but rather with analysis from an epistemological viewpoint.[61]

Dilthey's point here is crucial and it has often been overlooked. He is not proposing *Verstehen* as a psychological method which, if successfully applied to the analysis of events or human behaviour, claims to yield knowledge. Thus Dilthey denies claim (a), maintaining instead (c) that *Verstehen* represents an epistemological process. Claim (c) is important, particularly in the light of some of Dilthey's other claims, namely D4 that *Verstehen* constitutes the only way in which knowledge of human reality may be acquired, and D3 that the humanities must be regarded as having comparable cognitive worth as the natural sciences.

What is it that understanding comprehends? How does it yield knowledge? In the passage from the *Entwürfe* quoted in the paragraph above, Dilthey appears to be claiming (d) that *Verstehen* in its epistemological sense presupposes the possibility of *Verstehen* in its psychological sense. As correctly interpreted, *Verstehen* is a procedure which presupposes that people can enter into the thoughts and feelings, indeed the whole inner life, of other people empathetically, thereby rediscovering the I in the Thou.[62] That this psychological process is possible, that one person can reconstruct the inner life of another, Dilthey grounds in a notion of *der objective Geist* (objective mind).[63] But this empathetic activity, while presupposed by *Verstehen* in its epistemological sense, is not what Dilthey means by '*Verstehen*.'

In order to see what Dilthey means by '*Verstehen*,' it is important to ask: on what does *Verstehen* operate? What is the product of the method of *Verstehen*? Dilthey claims that the product of this process is knowledge, knowledge of Life (in Dilthey's sense of *das Leben*.) *Verstehen* is not, however, understanding *that* some event has occurred. Understanding is not concerned with *that* a marriage breakdown has occurred, for instance, or that people create eternal verities when confronted by the insecurities of an unstable hostile world. Nor is understanding concerned with *why* or *how* an event occurred, *i.e.*, with the causal or motivational factors in terms of which the event may be comprehended. Explanation is the appropriate mode of inquiry here, and this Dilthey would readily acknowledge. Discussion of *Verstehen* such as those defending or refuting claim (b) above have erred in treating the method of *Verstehen* as if it were just another way, an admittedly weaker way, of acquiring the same sort of knowledge that explanation (in Dilthey's sense of *Erklärung*) is capable of producing. *Verstehen*, however, is not more of the same sort of knowledge acquired differently. In Dilthey's judgment, it is the only way of acquiring knowledge about a different sort of experience. Thus claim (b) would have to be modified from a claim which views *Verstehen* as a process yielding knowledge of the sort capable of being obtained by explanation to a claim (e) that *Verstehen* is a process which yields knowledge about *das Leben* which is not otherwise obtainable in comprehending events of human concern.

*Verstehen*, as epistemologically interpreted, in Dilthey's intended sense, has to do with the significance or meaning of an event, action, or idea for some person or group of persons. It enables comprehension of what makes that event, action, or idea *bedeutsam* (significant). Understanding, in Dilthey's sense of the word, denotes a triadic relationship: *Verstehen* is (1) the significance of (2) some event, action, or idea (3) for someone. Too often Dilthey's notion of understanding has been treated as a binary relationship: a person understands such-and-such. This misconstrual has served only to conflate understanding with explanation in the manner of those who support or deny claim (b).

Understanding, then, is not incompatible with the use of explanation in the humanities as long as it is realized that both methods pertain to different sorts of experience and that explanation does not touch upon what is peculiarly the domain of the humanities. Consider, for instance, the event of the Exodus. When it happened and how it happened may be investigated historically; the circumstances under which Moses emerged as a leader and the means by which the captives escaped may be examined psychologically and sociologically. This much can be investigated by means of explanation. What is of interest to the humanities, however, and what prompts the use of *Verstehen* as a method, is the desire to comprehend the lived experience of this event: what it meant to the people to be liberated, what future they projected, and what it was about this event which constituted them as a people with an identity and shared experiences which they never had had before. It is with this aspect of the event, the significance of the event for the people that is accessible by means of the method of Verstehen and which constitutes the basis of what Dilthey regards as historical understanding.[64]

## 4. Hermeneutics: Verstehen and Allgemeingültigkeit

In *Die Entstehung der Hermeneutik* Dilthey makes the following claim:

> D5. *Verstehen* is "the sense in which, from signs given outwardly to the senses, we know an inner reality."[65]

Understanding, then, especially as applied to monuments of Life (*e.g.*, to texts, art forms, archaeological objects, *etc.*), moves from the expression of *Erlebnis* to *Erlebnis* itself. Understanding is a reconstructive epistemological process. All the humanities are based upon this movement. The process of *Verstehen*, however, cannot be just a private pleasurable savouring. While it is that, Dilthey points out also that "the whole of philological and historical knowledge is based on the presupposition that this understanding of the singular can be raised to the level of objectivity (*Allgemeingültigkeit*)."[66] This necessity, essentially what Dilthey claimed in D3, raises several problems for the humanities which Dilthey acknowledges at the beginning of *Die*

*Entstehung der Hemeneutik*. For one thing, how can the understanding of the singular be raised to the level of objective validity? For another, given that the reality with which the humanities is concerned is accessible only in inner experience, how can it be apprehended objectively? Finally, how can a consciousness with an individual make-up of its own achieve an objective knowledge of another and quite differently constituted individuality by means of the sort of reconstruction demanded by *Verstehen*?[67] These are fundamental questions for any theory of the humanities such as Dilthey's that would do justice to both D3 and D4.

The task of hermeneutics is to provide just such an account of the humanities, at least for those portions of the humanities which have to do with literary remains. Dilthey indicates that by 'exegesis' or 'interpretation' he means the skilled understanding of "permanently fixed expressions of Life," especially those contained in writing.[68] Hermeneutics, as the theory of textual interpretation, has the task of determining the possibility of a universally valid interpretation.[69] Dilthey agrees with Schleiermacher that hermeneutics concerns an analysis of understanding in general, but with this proviso: hermeneutics is to furnish an account of objectively valid understanding. At the end of *Die Entstehung der Hermeneutik* Dilthey offers this description of the hermeneutic task:

> D6. Hermeneutics is "to furnish, in opposition to the continual inroads of romantic arbitrariness and sceptical subjectivity into the field of history, a theoretical vindication of the universal validity of interpretation upon which all security in history depends."[70]

Hermeneutics becomes, then, the attempt to reconcile the demands of *Verstehen* with those of *Allgemeingültigkeit* for literary remains.

## 5. The Dilemma of Hermeneutics

The main strands of Dilthey's argument which lead to a dilemma can be summarized as follows:

> D1. There is an important distinction to be made between the humanities and the natural sciences.
>
> D2. Any attempt to develop a theory about the humanities must do justice to the sort of experience with which the humanities are properly concerned.
>
> D3. Any attempt to develop a theory about the humanities must do justice to the cognitive worth of the humanities.
>
> D4. D2 requires the recognition that the humanities employ a different mode of cognition than do the natural sciences.
>
> D5. *Verstehen* is "the process in which, from signs given outwardly to the senses, we know an inner reality."
>
> D6. Hermeneutics is "to furnish...a theoretical vindication of the universal validity of interpretation, upon which all security in history depends."

In general, the dilemma that Dilthey poses for hermeneutics and more broadly for any theory of the humanities arises out of the conflict that he notes in the

*Aufbau* between "the tendencies of life" and "the intellectual goals of the humanities."[71] The dilemma can be stated quite simply in the following form.

(1) D1, D2, D4 and D5 contend that hermeneutics and the theory of the humanities must explicitly recognize the peculiarities of the *Geisteswissenschaften*, their immersion in Life, and the necessity for comprehending them in terms of *das Verstehen*. This is what is distinctive about the humanities. As he says in the *Aufbau*, "a body of study belongs to the humanities only when its subject matter becomes accessible to us through an approach founded on the connection between Life, expression, and understanding."[72]

(2) D1, D3 and D6 maintain that hermeneutics and the theory of the humanities in general must establish a basis upon which the results of understanding in the humanities can be regarded as having objective validity. In the *Aufbau*, Dilthey points out that:

> Because historians, economists, teachers of law and students of religion stand in the midst of life they want to influence it. They subject historical personages, mass movements and tendencies to their judgment, which is conditioned by their individuality, the nation to which they belong and the age in which they live. Even when they believe that their work is not based on presuppositions they are determined by their horizon (*Gesichtskreis*); for every analysis of the concepts of a former generation reveals in them constituents which derive from the presupposition of that generation.[73]

In spite of this, Dilthey goes on to say:

> But, in every science as such the demand for general validity is implied. If the human studies are to be sciences

> in the strict sense of the word they must aim at validity
> more consciously and more critically.[74]

The importance of objective validity lies not only in ensuring the cognitive status of the humanities as intellectual disciplines. The effectiveness with which the humanities make an impact upon society depends, Dilthey contends, on "passing through the objectivity of scientific knowledge."[75]

(3) Since interpretation depends upon *Verstehen*, Dilthey in D6 maintains that hermeneutics or a theory of the humanities must do justice to D4 (*Verstehen*) *and* to D3 (*Allgemeingültigkeit*).

(4) But the considerations which underlie D2 would seem to rule out the possibility of D3. The reasons for this are apparent. D2 takes hermeneutics in the direction of *Verstehen* which in turn is seen as providing the only means of access to the kind of experience that gives rise to the humanities: *Erlebnis*, the spiritual world, the world of the historical. It is clear why Dilthey would want the results of investigation into the domain of experience to have objective validity. Yet at the same time it is tremendously difficult to see how objective validity is a concept at all applicable to this sort of experience. Dilthey, of course, recognized this difficulty, both at the beginning of *Die Entstehung der Hermeneutik* where he poses three fundamental questions for hermeneutic theory, mentioned in section 4 of this chapter, and also in the *Aufbau* where he indicates the impossibility of a presuppositionless understanding of a text. It may be that the requirement advanced by Dilthey in D3 is too strict for the humanities and represents an attempt to view the humanities from an explanatory point of view indicative of natural scientific proclivities. If this is the case, then the requirement that results in the humanities have objective validity is nothing more than a befuddled attempt to resuscitate a *natürliche* approach to the *Geisteswissenschaften*. If this is not the case, then it may be that "objective validity" is ambiguous, having one sense appropriate to explanation, and yet

another for understanding. If so, then it is not at all clear (a) what "objective validity" in this sense would mean, or (b) how such objective validity is possible, or even (c) how objective validity in this sense would ensure the comparable worth of the humanities with the natural sciences.

(5) Similarly, the considerations which underlie D3 would seem to rule out the possibility of D2, for reasons already indicated in (4).

Dilthey's dilemma is this: how can one maintain in one hermeneutic theory the requirements stated in both D2 *and* D3 when the considerations which underlie D2 and D3 appear to indicate that the theoretical options are either D2 *or* D3 but not both? Dilthey clearly intended to affirm both D2 *and* D3, although the basis upon which he attempted to resolve these two "tendencies" is far from clear.[76] Rather, it would seem as if these two tendencies are to be driven farther apart, into two poles of a thorny dilemma for hermeneutic theory.

For Dilthey any hermeneutic option which sacrificed either D2 or D3 would result in a truncated view of textual interpretation and would reduce the humanities either to a positivistic nightmare or to an idealistic dream. His dilemma, however, and the line of reasoning which supports it, sets the framework within which subsequent hermeneutic investigations have occurred.

## ENDNOTES

[1] There are problems translating this word into English but, as von Wright points out, "...it should be mentioned that the word was originally coined for the purpose of translating into German the English term 'moral science'." Von Wright further mentions that "The work which introduced the term *Geisteswissenschaften* appears to have been the translation of Mill's *Logic* by Schiel in 1863. Bk. VI of Mill 1843 is called in the translation 'Von der Logik der Geisteswissenschaften oder moralischen Wissenschaften.' It was Dilthey who made the term current." See G.I. von Wright, *Explanation and Understanding* (London: Routledge and Kegan Paul, 1971), pp. 6, 173. I have translated '*Geisteswissenschaften*' as "the humanities," partly to distinguish the *Geisteswissenschaften* from *Naturwissenschaften* and partly to allow ambiguity over the subject matter and methodology of the social sciences.

[2] For studies of the development of Dilthey's thought, see H.A. Hodges, *The Philosophy of Wilhelm Dilthey* (London: Routledge and Kegan Paul, 1952); Otto F. Bollnow, *Dilthey: Eine Einführung in seine Philosophie*, 2nd. ed. (Stuttgart: W. Kohlhammer, 1955); William Kluback, *Wilhelm Dilthey's Philosophy of History* (New York: Columbia University Press, 1956); Georg Misch, "Vorbericht des Herausgebers," in *Wilhelm Dilthey: Gesammelte Schriften*, (Stuttgart: B.G. Tuebner, 1961), pp. vii-cxvii; and H.N. Tuttle, *Wilhelm Dilthey's Philosophy of Historical Understanding* (Leiden: E.J. Brill, 1969). For a study of Dilthey's Kantianism, see H.A. Hodges, *op.cit.*, chapters 1-3. For a study of Dilthey's "Cartesian presuppositions," see H.-G. Gadamer, *op.cit.*, and Matthew Lamb, "Wilhelm Dilthey's critique of historical reason and Bernard Lonergan's meta-methodology," in Philip McShane (ed.), *op.cit.*, pp. 115-166.

[3] Note Tuttle, *op.cit.*, p. 5: "We will translate *Allgemeingültigkeit* as simply 'objective validity,' though the term refers also to the general or universal validity demanded of a science."

[4] Unless otherwise indicated, all textual references to Dilthey's writings will be to the volume and pages of the 1961 - Tuebner edition of *Wilhelm Dilthey: Gesammelte Schriften* (abbreviated here as *G.S.*). All translations from the German are mine, unless otherwise indicated.

[5] Originally published in 1883. Reprinted in *G.S.*, I.

[6] Originally published in 1900. Reprinted in *G.S.*, V, 317-338.

[7] These unpublished drafts were composed ca. 1907-1910. Printed in *G.S.*, VII, 191-291 where the editor, Bernhard Groethuysen, entitles them *"Plan der Fortsetzung zum Aufbau der Geschichtlichen Welt in den Geisteswissenschaften."*

[8] Originally published in 1910. Reprinted in *G.S.*, VII, 79-188.

[9] *Vorrede* was published in 1911, and reprinted along with three other essays which the editor entitled *"Autobiographisches"* in *G.S.*,, V. 3-27.

[10] *G.S.*, V, 3.

[11] On the difficulties in translating this phrase, see the Translator's Preface to Wolfhart Pannenberg, *Basic Questions in Theology*, I, translated by George H. Kehm (London: S.C.M. Press, 1970), pp. ix-xiv.

[12] *G.S.*, V, 4.

[13] *G.S.*, II, 1.

[14] *G.S.*, II, 498.

[15] *G.S.* For these three motifs, see "Die Grundmotive des metaphysischen Bewusstseins," *G.S.*, II, 494-499.

[16] *G.S.*, II, 494.

[17] See, for instance, his *Auffassung und Analyse des Menschen im 15, und 16, Jahrhundert, Das natürliche System der Geisteswissenschaften im 17, Jahrhundert,* and *Die Funktion der Anthropologie in der Kultur des 16, und 17, Jahrhunderts.*

[18] *G.S.*, I, 351-408.

[19] *Q.V.*, Horace L. Friess, "Wilhelm Dilthey," *The Journal of Philosophy* 26 (1929), pp. 14, 15.

[20]*Ibid.*, p. 15. Reconstructed from *G.S.*, I, 359-373.

[21]Wilhelm Dilthey, *The Essence of Philosophy*, translated by Stephen A. Emery and William T. Emery (Chapel Hill: University of North Carolina Press, 1954), p. 15.

[22]*Ibid.*

[23]Friess, *op cit.*, p. 16.

[24]*The Essence of Philosophy*, p. 23.

[25]See, for instance, *G.S.*, I, 379 or the essay entitled *Das Natürliche System der Geisteswissenschaften im 17. Jahrhundert*, G.S., II, 90-245.

[26]*G.S.*, V, 3.

[27]*Ibid.*

[28]*The Essence of Philosophy*, p. 15.

[29]*Ibid.*, p. 24. This theme was later on extensively developed by Husserl. See Edmund Husserl, *The Crisis of European Sciences and Transcendental Phenomenology*, translated by David Carr (Evanston: Northwestern University Press, 1970).

[30]H.A. Hodges, *op cit.*, p. 38. Tuttle notes that Dilthey uses *Erlebnis* and *das Erleben* interchangeably. See H.N. Tuttle, *op. cit.*, p. 16.

[31]*The Essence of Philosophy*, pp. 17, 18, 16.

[32]*G.S.*, V, 4.

[33]It would take us too far afield in this investigation, I think, to probe Dilthey's critique of empiricism in any critical detail. Such an examination would deal

centrally with two main works: *Ideen über eine beschreibende und zergliedernde Psychologie*, originally published in 1894 and reprinted in *G.S.*, V, 139-240, and *Studien zur Grundlegung der Geisteswissenschaften*, three studies of which the first was published in 1905 and reprinted in *G.S.*, VII, 3-75.

[34]Note here that Dilthey has not shown that the humanities have epistemological significance. Rather he is claiming that they ought to be so regarded.

[35]See, for example, discussion of this in *Die Einleitung in die Geisteswissenschaften, Entwürfe zur Kritik der historischen Vernunft*, and *Der Aufbau der Geschichtlichen Welt in den Geisteswissenschaften*.

[36]*G.S.*, VII, 191. Passage translated by H.P. Rickman, *Meaning in History* (London: George Allen and Unwin, 1961), p. 67.

[37]Friess, *op.cit.*, p. 9, *Cf.*, Peter Krausser, "Dilthey's Revolution in the Theory of the Structure of Scientific Inquiry and Rational Behavior," *Review of Metaphysics* 22 (1968-69), p. 264.

[38]*G.S.*, VII, 79.

[39]*Ibid.*

[40]*G.S.*, VII, 136.

[41]*G.S.*, VII, 205. *N.B.* There is only one method here.

[42]Cf. "Nature we explain; the forms of life (*Seelenleben*) we understand." From *Ideen über eine beschreibende und zergliedernde Psychologie* (1894). *G.S.*, V, 144.

[43]"According to the objects and according to the nature of human thinking, the three possible scientific methods are: the speculative, philosophically or theologically, the physical, and the historical. Their essence is to find out, to explain, to understand." Johann Gustav Droysen, *Outline of the Principles of History*, translated by E. Benjamin Andrews (New York: Howard Fertig, 1967), p. 15.

[44]In "Nature and History," Droysen contends that even if one presents a psychology of sex or a sociological analysis of marriage, there is still an essential aspect of marriage which defies such analysis: "Common remembrance of common experiences, possession of common hopes and cares, losses and successes, renew again even for couples who are growing old, the warmth of their first bliss. For them their marriage has a history. In this history its moral might was founded for them, and it is justified and fulfilled in and by the same." Droysen, *op.cit.*, Appendix II, p. 101.

[45]See Heinz Kimmerle, *op.cit.*, p. 107.

[46]Martin Redeker, *Schleiermacher: Life and Thought*, translated by John Wallhausser (Philadelphia: Fortress Press, 1973), p. 175.

[47]H. Kimmerle (ed.), *Fr. D.E. Schleiermacher: Hermeneutik* (Heidelberg: Carl Winter, 1959), p. 79.

[48]*Ibid.*, p. 80.

[49]For the importance of oral conversation upon Schleiermacher's hermeneutics, see Richard R. Niebuhr, "Schleiermacher on Language and Feeling," *Theology Today* 17 (1960-61), 150-167, and his *Schleiermacher on Christ and Religion* (New York: Charles Scribner's Sons, 1964), pp. 79ff. For a more general discussion, see Paul Ricoeur, "Qu'est-ce qu'un Texte," in R. Bubner, K. Cramer, R. Wiehl (eds.), *Hermeneutik und Dialektik* (Tübingen: J.C.B. Mohn (Paul Siebeck), 1970), vol. II, pp. 181-200 and translated by Paul Ricoeur as "What is a Text? Explanation and Interpretation," in David M. Rasmussen, *Mythic-Symbolic Language and Philosophical Anthropology* (The Hague: Nijhoff, 1971), pp. 135-150.

[50]Kimmerle (ed.), *Fr. D.E. Schleiermacher: Hermeneutik*, p. 56.

[51]*Ibid.*, p. 80.

[52]Niebuhr, *Schleiermacher on Christ and Religion*, pp. 82, 83.

[53]*Ibid.*, p. 80.

[54]Kimmerle (ed.), *Fr. D.E. Schleiermacher: Hermeneutik*, p. 87.

[55]See Kimmerle (ed.), *Fr. D.E. Schleiermacher: Hermeneutik*, p. 87. For others who have espoused this maxim, see Redeker, *op.cit.*, pp. 176, 177.

[56]*G.S.*, VII, 136. Passage translated by Rickman, *op. cit.*, p. 79.

[57]"*Verstehen*...is viewed by its proponents as a method by means of which we can explain human behavior." See Theodore Abel, "The Operation Called 'Verstehen'," *American Journal of Sociology* 54 (1948-49), 211-218 and reprinted in Edward H. Madden (ed.), *The Structure of Scientific Thought* (Boston: Houghton Mifflin, 1960), pp. 158-166 from which all references to Abel's article are taken. Note also Scriven's view of *Verstehen*: "...the doctrine that empathic insight was a special and valuable tool in the study of human behavior which was without counterpart in the physical sciences." Michael Scriven, "Logical Positivism and the Behavioral Sciences," in Peter Achinstein and Stephen F. Barker (eds.), *The Legacy of Logical Positivism* (Baltimore: The Johns Hopkins Press, 1969), p. 201.

[58]See Michael Scriven, "Causes, Connections and Conditions in History," in W.H. Dray (ed.), *Philosophical Analysis and History* (New York: Harper and Row, 1966), pp. 238-264; "Logical Positivism and the Behavioral Sciences," *Loc. cit.*; and "Verstehen Again, *Theory and Decision*" 1 (1971), 382-386.

[59]"Logical Positivism and the Behavioral Sciences," p. 201.

[60]T. Abel, *op. cit.*, p. 166. For other critics of *Verstehen*, see E. Zilsel, "Physics and the Problem of Historico-Sociological Laws," *Philosophy of Science* 8 (1941), 567-579; James W. Van Evra, "On Scriven on 'Verstehen'," *Theory and Decision* 1 (1971), 377-381. For qualified support of Scriven's defense of *Verstehen*, see Howard Cohen, "*Das Verstehen* and Historical Knowledge," *American Philosophical Quarterly* 10 (1973), 299-306 and Thomas McCarthy, "On Misunderstanding 'Understanding'," *Theory and Decision* 3 (1973), 351-370.

[61]*G.S.*, VII, 205. Passage translated by J.J. Kuehl in Patrick Gardiner (ed.), *Theories of History* (New York: The Free Press, 1959), p. 213.

[62]*G.S.*, VII, 191.

[63]See *G.S.*, VII, 208-210, H.A. Hodges, *op. cit.*, 264ff., and H.N. Tuttle, *op. cit.*, 34ff.

[64]*Verstehen* in either its psychological or epistomological sense poses many problems. For a consideration of some of these, see H.N. Tuttle, *op. cit.*, ch. VI.

[65]*G.S.*, V, 318.

[66]*G.S.*, V, 317.

[67]*G.S.*, V, 317, 318.

[68]*G.S.*, V, 319, 320.

[69]*G.S.*, V, 320.

[70]*G.S.*, V, 331. Passage translated by H.A. Hodges, *op. cit.*, p. 137. For a general discussion of what Dilthey means by *Allgemeingültigkeit*, see Tuttle, *op. cit.*, ch. 6, especially pp. 106ff.

[71]*G.S.*, VII, 137.

[72]*G.S.*, VII, 87.

[73]*G.S.*, VII, 137. Passage translated by Rickman, *op. cit.*, p. 81.

[74]*Ibid.*

[75]*Ibid.*

[76]See H.N. Tuttle, *op. cit.*, for a more detailed study of Dilthey's own sketch of a resolution to the dilemma.

# CHAPTER 3

# BULTMANN'S HERMENEUTICS: A CRITICAL EXAMINATION

Bultmann's hermeneutics has had an enormous impact on contemporary philosophy of religion. His position, however, contains some important confusions concerning the nature of textual interpretation that have clouded subsequent hermeneutics. In an attempt to inject a sense of analytic clarity into the discussion, this paper examines Bultmann's approach to hermeneutics, indicates the main lines of his hermeneutic solution, and offers a critical assessment of his position.

I argue that Bultmann confuses the scholarly and mediational purposes of interpretation, that he confuses the interpretation of an event with the interpretation of a text, and that he clouds the distinction between an interpretation of a text and the use to which an interpretation of a text can be put by an interpreter.

## 1. The Problem of Hermeneutics

In "The Problem of Hermeneutics,"[1] Bultmann proposes a reorientation of the roots of hermeneutics within the general framework for hermeneutics created by Schleiermacher and Dilthey. For them, the task of hermeneutics became the uncovering of the presuppositions of *Verstehen*, those that make understanding possible. While sympathetic to these hermeneutic aims, Bultmann contends, however, that they failed to characterize accurately what constitute the presuppositions of *Verstehen*. Schleiermacher and Dilthey grounded the possibility of textual understanding and all historical understanding generally on the affinity of the interpreter with the author. It is because of a communality among people reflective of what is true of human nature (Schleiermacher) or of Life (Dilthey) that understanding is rendered possible. It is, however, precisely the locating of the possibility of textual understanding in an interpreter-author affinity that Bultmann questions. He asks:

> Are we to suppose that the interpretation of a mathematical or medical text arises from the consummation of the psychical process which have been taking place in the author? Or do we only understand the inscriptions of the Egyptian kings telling of their deeds of war, or the ancient Babylonian and Assyrian historical and chronological texts, or the epitaph of Antiochus of Commagene or the Res Gestae Divi Augusti — do we understand them only on the basis of their translation into the inner, creative process in which they arose?[2]

The answer for Bultmann is clear: the understanding of such texts does not depend on any bond of affinity between interpreter and author. Such texts may be read as expressions of Life (in Dilthey's sense), and Bultmann acknowledges this possibility, but they are more apt to be read, he maintains, for what they have to say directly about mathematical or medical knowledge or the events of world history.

If this is the case, then certain important consequences follow. For one thing, the view of Schleiermacher and Dilthey is "one-sided"[3] and misleading. It cannot be the case that "reflection on the individuality of author and expositor, on their psychical processes and on the spiritual make-up or intellectual consanguinity of the expositor"[4] constitutes the presuppositions of understanding. Rather the crucial presupposition of textual understanding is the relationship of the interpreter in his life to the subject matter about which the author speaks. It is this relationship and not interpreter-author affinity which makes textual understanding possible. Thus Bultmann makes the following claim, which for ease of subsequent reference will be called "B1":

> B1. The presupposition for understanding is the interpreter's relationship in his life to the subject which is directly or indirectly expressed in the text.[5]

Because the interpreter is vitally interested in what the text has to say about the subject matter, he approaches it in a specific manner. The purposes the interpreter has in examining the text, purposes developed out of his own living experience, guide his interpretation of the text. They motivate his inquiry into its meaning and give his inquiry specific shape. Bultmann also notes that the interpreter's approach to textual understanding "is governed always by a prior understanding (*Vorverständnis*) of the subject."[6] Without such prior understanding, no question, and, consequently, no interpretation of the text is possible. More generally, Bultmann claims:

> B2. Every interpretation incorporates a particular prior understanding — namely, that which arises out of the context of living experience to which the subject belongs.[7]

Of all Bultmann's claims, B2 is particularly open to misconstrual. It is important to note (1) the extent to which every interpretation *incorporates (einschliessen)* a particular understanding, and (2) exactly what prior understanding is understanding of. By "prior understanding" Bultmann does not mean to indicate that the interpreter imposes upon the text his own idea of what the text must mean, for this would serve to render the text negligible in interpretation.[8] Nor by "prior understanding" does he mean a preliminary understanding of what the text means, *i.e.*, an initial, exploratory, and yet revisable comprehension of the text's meaning, the sort of understanding that might be gained from a first reading of the text. Similarly, dogmatic prejudices concerning what the text ought to disclose do not constitute prior understanding.[9] Thus by way of summary Bultmann claims:

> B3. By "prior understanding" is not meant any of the following:
> a) the interpreter's understanding of what the text means;
> b) the interpreter's preliminary and revisable understanding of what the text might mean; or
> c) the interpreter's conviction of what the text ought to mean.

Prior understanding is the interpreter's grasp of the subject matter with which the text deals and not his comprehension of the meaning of the text *per se*. Moreover, Bultmann claims, such prior understanding is necessary if true understanding of the text is to occur. Without it, the interpreter would not sense with immediacy and vitality the questions with which the author of the text strove. As Bultmann says:

> It is evident that the questioning arises from a particular interest in the matter referred to, and therefore that a particular understanding of the matter is presupposed. I like to call this a *pre-understanding*.[10]

Thus Bultmann maintains the following position:

> B4. Understanding a text presupposes a prior understanding on the part of the interpreter, a prior understanding indicative of his own understanding in his life of the subject matter with which the text under examination deals, which prompts his questioning of the text, and which reflects his particular purpose in investigating the text.

Bultmann's claim, then, concerning the role of prior understanding in textual interpretation is not at all like Plato's claim in the Meno that in some sense one must already know if inquiry is to be possible, nor like Bardaisan's claim in *The Book of the Laws of the Countries* that one must already believe if true knowledge is to be attained.[11]

Even though prior understanding is not understanding of the text, Bultmann maintains that it plays an important role in the understanding of textual meaning. In B4 the role ascribed by Bultmann to prior understanding is that of initiating inquiry. In B2, however, in spite of what is maintained in B3(a), the role assigned prior understanding appears to be much more substantive: as he says, "every interpretation *incorporates* a particular prior understanding." To what extent, then, does prior understanding influence or in some way dictate the results of exegesis — in spite of what Bultmann asserts in B3(a)? Claims B2 and B4 leave open the question: do different interpretive purposes result in different exegetical results? If so, then to some extent different purposes and interests would influence the varying interpretive results, and consequently prior understanding would play a substantially different role than the one explicitly assigned to it. This consequence is regarded by some as a serious threat to interpretive objectivity.

Karl Barth, for instance, asks the following:

> Is it possible to understand any text, be it ancient or modern, if we approach it with preconceived notions about the extent and the limit to which it can be understood? Is it not preferable to come to it with an open mind and patiently follow what it has to say?...Surely, if we want to understand any given text, the provisional clue to its understanding must be sought from the text itself, and moreover from its spirit, content and aim.[12]

And in a similar vein, in introducing his *Christology of the New Testament*, Oscar Cullmann writes:

> I emphasize here only that I know no other 'method' than the proven philological-historical one. I know of no other 'attitude' toward the text than obedient willingness to listen to it even when what I hear is sometimes completely foreign, contradictory to my own favorite ideas, whatever they may be; the willingness at least to take the trouble to understand and present it, regardless of my own philosophical and theological 'opinions'; and above all the willingness to guard against designating a biblical statement a dispensable 'form' because it is unacceptable to me on the basis of my opinions.[13]

Both Barth and Cullmann interpret Bultmann's claims B2 and B4 as erecting a hermeneutic which tends to legitimize both the interpreter's reading into the text his own preconceptions concerning what it ought to mean and as exempting the interpreter from the difficult but necessary task of bracketing his own preconceptions and of listening to what the text has to say. In spite of Bultmann's claim B3, there is considerable textual warrant for Barth's and Cullmann's interpretation of the implications of Bultmann's position, e.g., the vagueness of 'incorporates' in B2 and the possibility left open in B4 that different interpretive purposes may result in different interpretive results. There are further grounds in the examples of interpretive purposes and prior understanding at work in textual understanding provided in "The Problem of Hermeneutics."

Bultmann's examples of different types of interpretive interests would appear to substantiate the claim that interpretive results are at least to some degree guided or determined by interpretive purposes. With respect to history, for example, Bultmann argues:

> Each historical phenomenon can be seen from different points of view.... The historical judgment may be guided by psychological or ethical interest and also by aesthetic interest. Each of these different views is open to one side of this historical process, and from each viewpoint something objectively true will appear. The picture is falsified only if one single viewpoint is made an absolute one, if it comes to be a dogma.[14]

It would appear that Bultmann allows the possibility that interpreters with different types of interests will understand the same text differently and even that interpreters within each type of interest who hold different views of the subject matter will interpret texts differently. This does not indicate that interpretation is just the result of the interpreter's initial interest; nor does it indicate that an interpreter can just make the text mean what he wants it to mean. It does indicate, however, that the role which Bultmann ascribes to prior understanding is considerably more than one which simply serves to initiate the interpretive inquiry: it serves to guide the interpreter to a particular sort of understanding of the text. Indeed, something like this must occur if the purposes of existential understanding are to be realized. With respect to history, for example, Bultmann points out (as had Dilthey before him) that understanding history involves not just the determination of what occurs but also an assessment of its significance: "The judgment of importance depends on the subjective point of view of the historian."[15] Bultmann emphasizes that this recognition of the historian's subjectivity does not mitigate historical objectivity. It does serve, however, to indicate a much more substantive role for prior understanding than the one explicitly acknowledged by Bultmann and, furthermore, to indicate that at least indirectly interpretive purposes do influence interpretive results. Thus it would seem that B4 does not leave open the question concerning the relationship between different prior understandings and different exegetical conclusions.

If this is the case, then in spite of Bultmann's clear insistence on wanting to maintain B2, B3 and B4, it would appear that B2 and B3(a) are incompatible: one and only one of these claims can be upheld consistently. Yet it is difficult to discern which of these two Bultmann would forfeit. If B3(a) were forfeited, then Barth's and Cullmann's objections would be sustained, and Bultmann's hermeneutics would provide a substantial threat to interpretive objectivity. Yet Bultmann clearly would not be willing to forego B3(a). For Bultmann also makes the following important claim:

> B5. It is necessary in textual interpretation for the interpreter to be examined by the text and to hear the claim it makes.[16]

Similarly he writes:

> Real understanding would, therefore, be paying heed to the question posed in the work which is to be interpreted, to the claim which confronts one in the work, and the 'fulfillment' of one's own individuality would consist in the richer and deeper opening up of one's own possibilities — in being called forth out of one's self...by the work.[17]

Bultmann's claim B5 rejects any role for prior understanding within textual interpretation which would authorize imputation to a text of the interpreter's own conception of what it could or should mean, or which would suggest that prior understanding functions in such a way as to act as an impediment to an accurate discernment of what the text means.

On the other hand, if B2 and B4 were forfeited, then the existential quality of textual understanding would be undermined, and this, for Bultmann, would eliminate an essential ingredient in interpretation which truly aims at understanding. The dilemma is unresolvable at this point. The dilemma focuses on the antithesis between the impetus of prior understanding and the necessity for the interpreter "to be examined by the text" and to hear "the claim it makes;" between B2 and B4 on the one hand, and B3 and B5 on the other. Does not the hearing of the message of the text require at least to some extent a nullification of the interpreter's prior understanding of the subject matter, how can it be truly heard by a person with a quite different prior understanding?

If prior understanding were such that it occupied solely the role ascribed to it by Bultmann in B4, then in the light of B5, these questions would pose no problem. But if B4 is correctly construed as authorizing a much more substantial role for prior understanding, then even in spite of B5 these problems are unresolved. What is the relationship between the interpreter's prior understanding and the eventual interpretation he assigns a text? How reliable are the results obtained in textual interpretation which explicitly acknowledges the importance of prior understanding?

## 2. Bultmann's Hermeneutic Method

Bultmann's criterion for a successful hermeneutic can be summarized as follows:

> B6. An adequate hermeneutic approach ought to

> accommodate both (a) the role of prior understanding in textual interpretation [B2, B4], and also (b) the necessity of allowing the interpreter to be examined by the text and to hear the claim it makes [B5].

In a series of works devoted to the means by which texts (particularly but not exclusively biblical texts) can be demythologized,[18] Bultmann offers a hermeneutic approach which would satisfy B6. Demythologizing a text is a means whereby the "kerygma" of the text can be freed from its original mythological setting and made intelligible to readers today.

For Bultmann, the New Testament kerygma is "the proclamation of the decisive act in Christ."[19] This is its essential message which the composers of the original New Testament texts sought to render intelligible in patterns of thought with which they and their original readers were familiar. In general, the kerygma of a text is its original message presented with all the vividness, impact, and significance which attended its original proclamation. The significance dimension to the presentation of kerygma is important, especially for New Testament kerygma which calls for a response or a decision. For this reason kerygma can never be adequately treated as dull antiquarian stuff devoid of human significance. It can never be merely textual. As Bultmann writes to Jaspers, the real hermeneutic problem is

> the problem of interpreting the Bible and the teachings of the Church in such a way that they may become understandable as a summons to man.[20]

Myth, for Bultmann, has as its purpose "to express man's understanding of himself in the world in which he lives."[21] It "intends to speak of a reality beyond what can be objectified, observed, and controlled, and that is of decisive significance for human existence."[22] Mythology is thus a historically conditioned mode of expression which attempts to portray the significance of some event or person for some particular group: "in the last resort mythological language is only a medium for conveying the significance of the historical (*historisch*) event."[23] In general, myth is the mode of expression in which the message of a text (kerygma) is embedded; it serves to indicate the significance of the event or person for human life in general. Thus any attempt to do justice to the kerygma of the text must also do justice to the mythological mode of expression in which the kerygma is embedded and which serves as the primary means by which the significance of the kerygma is expressed.

The New Testament kerygma is set within the framework of Jewish apocalyptic and Gnostic redemption mythology. This mythological view of the world is "obsolete,"[24] alien to the view of contemporary biblical exegetes. This raises problems for the understanding of biblical texts. If the kerygma of the New Testament is embedded in mythological language, and if this mythological mode of expression is obsolete and alien to modern interpreters, then is the kerygma itself also obsolete and alien and thus devoid of significance, or can the kerygma be resuscitated in some adroit hermeneutical fashion? Bultmann asks:

> Can the kerygma be interpreted apart from mythology? Can we recover the truth of the kerygma for men who do not think in mythological terms without forfeiting its character as kerygma?[25]

Bultmann discuss several ways of dealing with this particular exegetical problem:

B7. There are four possible hermeneutic procedures with respect to texts whose kerygma is embedded in obsolete mythology:

(1) the interpreter may attempt to make sense of the kerygma in terms of its original mythological setting.

Such a procedure would not disassociate the kerygma from its mythological matrix: the meaning of the text is its mythological kerygma.

This hermeneutic procedure is unacceptable for several reasons. For one thing, this method would force acceptance of the mythological mode of expression in which the kerygma is embedded along with the kerygma itself. This is detrimental to the understanding and responding to the kerygma. Where the mythology is alien to contemporary patterns of thought, this procedure renders the kerygma itself "incredible," "unintelligible," or "unacceptable" to modern man.[26] Secondly, Bultmann maintains, it is senseless to expect contemporary interpreters to accept this mythological view of the world as true. It is simply "the cosmology of a pre-scientific age."[27] There is no reason why understanding and responding to the kerygma of the text necessitate acceptance of its mythological view of the world. Thirdly, it is impossible, Bultmann asserts, for interpreters today to adopt this worldview, "because no man can adopt a view of the world by his own volition — it is already determined for him by his place in history."[28] Furthermore, Bultmann points out, "It is no longer possible for anyone seriously to hold the New Testament view of the world — in fact, there is no one who does."[29]

The New Testament mythology stands as a barrier to the contemporary reader's understanding and acceptance of the kerygma. The interpreter brings to his reading of the text a critique of its mythological view of the world. Its view of the world is unacceptable to him because of its obsolescence: it is no longer a view of the world that is shared today. Much more importantly, it is unacceptable because such a view of the world no longer makes sense of the world as interpreters today understand it, and therefore, it cannot serve as a vehicle for portraying the significance of events. The mythology is unacceptable because it is unintelligible to people today. In sum, Bultmann's rejection of B7(1) is this:

> B8. Because the mythology of the New Testament is obsolete, unacceptable, and unintelligible to people today, B7(1) renders the kerygma unintelligible.

Therefore B7(1) is to be rejected. A second hermeneutic option is:

> B7. (2) The interpreter eliminates the myth and kerygma of the original text, putting in its place a more acceptable meaning.

While no interpreter would probably set out to do this intentionally, in Bultmann's estimation this is precisely what happened within liberal Protestantism (e.g., in Harnack's work). In Bultmann's view, this movement eliminated not only the original mythology but also the kerygma, putting in its stead some moral or sociological truth thought to be compatible with the original text. This hermeneutic procedure simply fails to be interpretation. Interpretation cannot occur if a text is de-kerygmatized. The kerygma at least must be preserved.

A third hermeneutic option goes as follows:

> B7. (3) The interpreter eliminates (or ignores) the kerygmatic aspect of the text and examines only the mythology.

While Bultmann acknowledges that proponents of this hermeneutic approach, for example, the History of Religions movement, uncovered many interesting aspects of New Testament mythology, such a hermeneutic fails to constitute textual interpretation because, like B7(2), it eliminates the kerygma.

Finally,

> B7. (4) An interpreter demythologizes the text, preserving the kerygma.

In Bultmann's view, only B7(4) satisfies the requirements of B6: by preserving the kerygma it satisfies B6(b) for it allows the interpreter to hear the claim the text makes; by demythologizing, it satisfies B6(a), allowing the prior understanding the interpreter has of the world to be preserved intact. Thus for Bultmann B7(4) represents the appropriate hermeneutic method for the interpretation of such texts.[30]

It should be noted that demythologizing does not mean that the myth is not taken seriously, or is to be discounted or disregarded: on the contrary, it is to be used in a certain way. To the extent possible, given the difficulties concerning the intelligibility of obsolete mythology mentioned in B8, the interpreter must seek to interpret the myth so as to comprehend the reality and the significance to which it points.

It should also be noted that B7(4) is recommended by Bultmann not to make the New Testament palatable to modern man by the excision of certain difficult portions of the text (as Jaspers thought): it is adopted to make the kerygma intelligible to contemporary readers.[31] As Macquarrie notes, "Indeed, the whole aim of Bultmann's demythologizing is to set the kerygma free so that we may be genuinely addressed by it."[32] Similarly Ogden observes:

> It is widely supposed that Bultmann's real reason for proposing to demythologize the church's traditional

proclamation is the exigency of the present apologetic situation, in which Christians are required to witness to a "scientific" world. From his own repeated statements on the matter, however, it is evident that this exigency is not at all the cause of his proposal, but simply its occasion. For him, the only final reason why demythologization is either possible or necessary is "faith itself" or, in other words, the understanding of God and man that has been developed....We must set aside all specifically "mythological" formulations because they completely obscure the fact that God's difference from the world is not merely "quantitative" but "qualitative." Therefore...the only way in which one can possibly do justice to Bultmann's own understanding of "demythologization" is to see it as a direct implication of his fundamental view of God and the world.[33]

## 3. Bultmann's Hermeneutics: A Critical Assessment

Several major observations will be made on Bultmann's argument as a whole.

**1.** B7(4) presupposes B7(1). That this is so can be seen from the following considerations. First of all, in keeping with Bultmann's own exposition of B7(4), the mythological matrix in which the kerygma of the text is set is not to be ignored: it is to be interpreted. The mythology plays an essential role in enabling the interpreter to understand the kerygma itself, to assess the sort of significance it had for its original hearers/readers, and to determine what current mode of thought might appropriately reembody the kerygma. Secondly, if this is so, then the interpreter must be able to understand the kerygma in terms of its original mythological format. This is precisely what B7(1) demands. Thus B7(4) presupposes B7(1).

**2.** Claim B8 plays an ambivalent role in Bultmann's argument. If observation (1) is correct, then B8 poses some major problems for the possibilities of textual understanding. If it is the case that kerygma of the text is set within "unintelligible imagery,"[34] as B8 maintains it is, then difficult questions are raised concerning how even an adroit interpreter could penetrate the mysteries of the mythological mode of expression so as to open up for understanding the full import of the kerygma itself. If B8 were taken *au pied de la lettre* in this fashion, then B7(1) would be impossible for anyone. Consequently, so would B7(4). This would constitute a disastrous consequence for the interpretation of texts whose kerygma is embedded within obsolete mythology.

Bultmann clearly does not intend an interpretive impasse. It may be that B8 ought to be construed as a constraint upon the ordinary person seeking understanding of the biblical message today and not the interpreter as such. It may be that the ordinary person cannot fathom the mythology in which the New Testament is placed while the interpreter by dint of expertise and scholarship can serve to mediate between the two domains and so preserve the kerygma intact. On this generous construal of B8, for which there is little textual warrant, B8 would not serve to exempt the interpreter from B7(1) but would serve to make the execution of this essential task all the more difficult. If textual understanding is to occur, then in spite of the severity of B8, someone, *i.e.*, the interpreter, must be able to comprehend the text's "unintelligible" mythology.

Favorably viewed, B8 at the very least creates difficulties for the execution of B7(1) and thus for B7(4). On the other hand, B8 is the claim on which Bultmann establishes the necessity of moving beyond the interpretive results of B7(1) to those of B7(4). B8 indicates the ways in which the hermeneutical procedure of B7(1) would issue forth in an unacceptable kerygma. Consequently, the results of B7(1) are not to be accepted as final but must be used by the interpreter to reexpress the kerygma in a way that indicates to modern man its significance and confronts him with the *skandalon*[35] of the message. Thus B8, in addition to creating difficulties for accomplishing B7(1) and consequently B7(4), necessitates that the interpreter move from the results of B7(1) to those of B7(4) if interpretation is to serve the purposes Bultmann intends.

**3.** Bultmann appears to demand that textual interpretation fulfil two major functions. That this is so can be seen first of all from a distinction between the interpreter and those for whom his interpretation is intended (in the case of biblical interpretation, "modern man") and secondly from the role Bultmann assigns the interpreter. For one thing, it is not mandatory that everyone who seeks an understanding of the Bible be able to accomplish the heroic hermeneutical feat required by B7(1): it is a requirement for the interpreter and not necessarily for those to whom his interpretation is offered. The interpreter serves as a mediator of the text's meaning for someone else: he stands between the text and those who are to receive his interpretation. The interpreter is like the great high priest who ascends to the repository of the mysteries and conveys them to those unqualified to enter that domain. Or, more simply, the interpreter is like the Protestant preacher whose role is the study of scripture and the exposition of its message for those who lack the expertise accurately to grasp it. Macquarrie draws attention to the dual responsibility of the interpreter:

> Barth asks: "To whom is the exegete responsible? To the presuppositions of the thought of himself and his contemporaries, to a canon of understanding formed by these; or to the statements of the text which are to be understood, to the canon yielded by the spirit, content and intention of the text itself?" One implication of this question is presumably that Bultmann makes himself responsible to the presuppositions of modern thought rather than to the statements of the New Testament. But

another more important implication contained in the question is that the exegete is faced with a choice. It is suggested that either he must make himself responsible to the outlook of those to whom his interpretation is addressed or he must make himself responsible to the outlook of the text which is being interpreted. But this is not the case. We have contended that a genuine interpretation has a responsibility to both sides at once.[36]

B7(4), then, does not represent an alternative to B7(1) but an extension of it designed to mediate the results of the latter to those who are not in a position to comprehend the kerygmatic significance of its exegetical results. From an apologetic point of view, because of B8, the interpretive results of B7(1) are unacceptable: they pose an unnecessary burden to the ordinary person interested in ascertaining the text's message; they needlessly obfuscate the kerygma. A hermeneutic procedure which simply represented the results of B7(1) to those for whom the interpretation is intended would impede the mediating function of textual interpretation. The interpreter would cease to be interpreting for somebody.

For Bultmann, textual interpretation would appear to comprise two major functions: (a) the scholarly one of establishing what the text originally meant (its original kerygma and myth) and (b) the mediating one of relating that meaning to those for whom the interpretation is made in the form that preserves intact the kerygma and its significance. Fulfilment of function (a) necessitates the interpreter's accomplishing B7(1); fulfilment of (b), however, demands that the interpreter use the results of B7(1) along the lines of B7(4).

**4.** B8 escalates the claims of B2 and B4. There is a major discrepancy between the claims made in B2 and B4 on the one hand and B8 on the other. First of all, in keeping with Bultmann's expositions of them, B2 and B4 are relatively innocuous claims and from them not much of theoretical interest ought to follow. Secondly, as was pointed out in section 1 above, there is some textual justification for the view that in practice Bultmann means much more by "prior understanding" than simply the interpreter's knowledge of the subject matter which initiates inquiry into the text meaning. It appears that the interpreter's interest in the text, his knowledge and beliefs about its subject matter, play a substantial role in the interpretation the text is ultimately given.

It is this alteration of B2 and B4 that paves the way for B8. For, thirdly, the augmented role of prior understanding on the part of the interpreter becomes escalated in B8 into a contention that because of the interpreter's views of the structure of the world and its possibilities, it becomes impossible for him to appreciate the significance of the kerygma embedded in obsolete mythological framework. The interpreter's own beliefs constitute an impediment to his understanding of the text: they stand as a shield between the text and his understanding of it. B8 demands that the interpreter make the text intelligible to those who hear or read his interpretation.

B8 is a crucial premise in Bultmann's argument advocating demythologizing. B8 is the major reason why Bultmann rejects B7(1) which could not be rejected solely on the grounds of either B2 or B4. There is nothing incompatible between B7(1) and B2 and B4 as originally intended by Bultmann. Thus B8 escalates the claims of B2 and B4. It represents a major turning point in Bultmann's thought.

**5.** It follows from B8 that the interpreter's understanding of the event about which a text speaks is allowed to influence his interpretation of the text itself. How this comes about, and the consequences which this implication of B8 bears for textual interpretation, can be seen from the following considerations.

A distinction may be made between (a) interpreting what a text means, and (b) interpreting the event about which the text reports. Exegesis usually denotes (a), for the interpreter's only access to the event (other than having been present at the event) is through the text itself or through some other text of the same event. Bultmann is concerned not just with (a) but also with (b). This concern is evident, for instance, in B1 where Bultmann maintains that the interest the interpreter has in the subject matter of the text constitutes the bond of affinity between interpreter and author. In accordance with B1, the interpreter approaches the text with a view to determining what it says about the event or subject matter. Thus, right from B1, the hermeneutic focus is on what the text says about the event.

Bultmann's concern with (b) is shown, moreover, in his discussion of heaven-hell cosmology, demon possession, miracles, angels, and the resurrection, for what contemporary readers believe possible today about such events or portrayals guides their understanding of texts dealing with such matters.[37] It is because contemporary persons seeking understanding of the biblical message come to the text equipped with a view of the structure of the world and its possibilities, and because this contemporary understanding of these differs from the original understanding of them, that the intelligibility of events posed in the original composer of the text's interpretation of the event is disallowed. No contemporary interpreter can understand the event as the original composer of the text understood it (although Bultmann intends to preserve the same kerygma and the same significance now as then).

According to B8, the recurrence of the original mythology of the text is unacceptable in interpretation because it embodies a view of the world which the interpreter (or those for whom his interpretation is intended) do not and cannot accept. Thus Bultmann is making two additional claims based on B8. The first concerns the nature of interpreting an event: the event, as initially interpreted by the composer of the text, need not be interpreted in that fashion today, and must not be, if anything of contemporary value is to be salvaged. The second claim involves the relationship between interpreting an event and interpreting a text which reports that event: the interpretation of texts ought to be guided by the interpreter's beliefs concerning the events about which the text speaks.

**6.** It may be the case that B7(4) fails to satisfy the conditions of B6. According to Bultmann, there would seem to be three phases involved in demythologizing a text. Initially the interpreter must understand the original text — in Bultmann's terms, understand its kerygma (call this "$K_1$") and its mythological format (call this "$M_1$"). In effect, this phase of B7(4) requires the interpreter to undertake B7(1). Next, from this the interpreter must extract the text's essential message and significance. If the demythologized and as yet unremythologized message be called "the nuclear kerygma" (same as $K_1$ but understood independently of $M_1$), and if the significance of the kerygma for its initial audience as indicated by $M_1$ be called "the nuclear significance," then the second phase involves the isolation of the nuclear kerygma and the nuclear significance from the kerygma and mythology of the original.

This second phase of demythologizing itself involves certain crucial problems: *e.g.*, (i) the differentiation of what is mythological from what is kerygmatic, and (ii) the extent to which the kerygma is detachable and comprehensible independently of mythology. Finally, the nuclear kerygma ($K_1$) must be reexpressed in some contemporary mode of expression (call this "$M_2$") which preserves the same significance for $K_1$ as did $M_1$. Without preservation of significance, the kerygma would fail to be expressed with the same sort of vitality, urgency and decision-provoking power that attended the kerygma in its initial proclamation. Thus, for Bultmann, B7(4) respects the contentions expressed in B8 and satisfies B6(a), by transposing $M_1$ into $M_2$ while retaining the same significance, and satisfies B6(b), by retaining throughout the process $K_1$.

What is problematic, however, is whether $K_1$ is indeed retained throughout his hermeneutic transaction, and whether $M_2$ expresses the same significance for hearers or readers today as $M_1$ did originally. These are problematic because of the comprehensive impediment to the understanding of obsolete mythology maintained by Bultmann in B8. Unless modified in some manner, B8 affirms the impenetrability of alien modes of expression, especially concerning kerygmatic significance. In the light of B8, it becomes doubtful that $K_1$ can be retained and that $M_2$ expresses the same kerygmatic significance as $M_1$.

In addition, in the light of observation (5) in which the interpreter's understanding of the event the text reports is allowed to influence the sort of textual interpretation that is acceptable and intelligible, maintenance of the same kerygma with the same significance becomes all the more unlikely. The kerygma would be modified by what the interpreter believes possible about the event in question, given his view of the nature of the world and the sorts of events that are likely to occur in it. Similarly the mythology and the significance to which it points would become altered by the interpreter's own dismissal of that mode of expression as utterly fantastic and impossible. In the light of what is believed by interpreters to be true of the world and of human experience, it is unlikely that the same message and the same significance would be conveyed.

If this is the case, then because of B8 and observation (5), B7(4) cannot satisfy the requirements of B6. Thus Bultmann's hermeneutic solution fails to satisfy the requirements for an adequate hermeneutic.

7. Bultmann confuses textual interpretation with the uses to which an interpretation of a text may be put. That this is so can be seen from the following consideration. As was shown in observation (3) above, Bultmann demands that textual interpretation fulfil two major functions. The first function is the scholarly one of establishing what the text originally meant: its original kerygma and myth. The second function is the mediating one of relating that meaning to those for whom the interpretation is intended in a manner that preserves the original kerygma and significance. The first function is related to the interpretation of the text; the second function, however, is related to a purpose to which the interpretation of the text may be put. One purpose to which an

interpretation of a text may be put is that of rendering it intelligible to those who lack access to scholarly means or else who hold a view of the world different from that portrayed in the text under interpretation. Furthermore, as was also pointed out in observation (3), B7(1) relates to the first task, and B7(4) to the second. Thus B7(1) would relate to textual interpretation and B7(4) to a special use to which the interpretation of the Bible may be put. If this were the case, the many of the problems to which Bultmann's thought falls heir could be surmounted. The two functions of textual interpretation could be accommodated, interpreter's interests recognized, and the mediating role of the interpreter given an important dimension. Yet trouble occurs because Bultmann rejects B7(1) because of B8 and advocates B7(4) as the only appropriate exegetical method for biblical interpretation. In making this claim, Bultmann has conflated the necessity of giving the Bible an interpretation with the desirability of using this interpretation in such a way that the Bible becomes intelligible to people today. The desire to provide an account of textual interpretation which would accomplish the mediating function Bultmann contends is so necessary obliterates the very basis upon which textual interpretation is possible. As observation (1) points out, B7(4) presupposes B7(1). It is only on the basis of B7(1) that the mediating function and the specific use to which Bultmann wishes to put the interpretation of a text is possible. And yet it is this very basis that Bultmann's hermeneutic disallows.

Because of the internal difficulties B8 occasions for Bultmann's hermeneutics and because of its lack of support in interpretive practice, B8 ought to be rejected. This leaves intact moderate claims concerning the relationship between the interpreter's prior understanding and the interpretation given the text, B2 and B4, and these claims are compatible with hermeneutic option B7(1). Forfeiting B8 would have the additional advantage of eliminating the basis upon which B7(1) was rejected by Bultmann. Furthermore, if the distinction between an interpretation of the text and the uses to which an interpretation of a text may be put is accepted, then B7(1) is related to the former and B7(4) to the latter. Thus, to a considerable extent both the content and intent of Bultmann's approach to hermeneutics would be preserved.

## ENDNOTES

[1]"The Problem of Hermeneutics," in Rudolph Bultmann, *Essays Philosophical and Theological* (London: SCM Press, 1955), pp. 234-261, reprinted in Barrie A. Wilson, *About Interpretation* (New York: Peter Lang, 1989). Originally published as "Das Problem der Hermeneutik," *Zeitschrift für Theologie und Kirche* (1950), 47-69 and reprinted in *Glauben und Verstehen*, II (Tübingen: J.C.B. Mohr, 1965), pp. 211-235.

[2]*Ibid.*, pp. 238-239. See also R. Bultmann, *History and Eschatology* (New York; Harper and Row, 1962) p. 112.

[3]"The Problem of Hermeneutics," p. 239.

[4]*Ibid.*

[5]*Ibid.*, p. 241. Italicized in original.

[6]*Ibid.*, p. 239. Italicized in original.

[7]*Ibid.*, pp. 241-242.

[8]"Is Exegesis without Presuppositions Possible?" in *Existence and Faith: Shorter Writings of Rudolf Bultmann,* selected, translated and introduced by Schubert M. Ogden (New York: World Publishing Co., 1960), p. 289.

[9]*Ibid.*, p. 290.

[10]*History and Eschatology,* p. 113. Cf. "...a specific understanding of the subject matter of the text, on the basis of a "life-relation" to it, is always presupposed by exegesis; and insofar as this is so exegesis is without presuppositions. I speak of this understanding as a 'pre-understanding'." "Is Exegesis without Presuppositions Possible?" p. 294.

[11]Plato, *Meno* 80D-8-D; H.J.W. Drijvers, *The Book of the Laws of the Countries* (Assen: Van Gorcum, 1965), pp. 7,8.

[12] Karl Barth, "Rudolf Bultmann - An Attempt to Understand Him," in Hans-Werner Bartsch (ed.), *Kerygma and Myth*, vol. II (London: S.P.C.K., 1962), p. 108.

[13] Oscar Cullmann, *The Christology of the New Testament* (Philadelphia: Westminster Press, 1959), p. xiv. Cullmann had already made a similar point in an earlier article, "Les problèmes posés par la méthode exégetique de l'école de Karl Barth," *Revue d'Histoire et de Philosophie Religieuses* 8 (1928), 70-83. For a discussion of some of the presuppositions of Cullmann's and Barth's exegetical methods, see Andre Malet, *The Thought of Rudolf Bultmann* (Garden City, N.Y.: Doubleday and Co., 1971), pp. 191-197.

[14] *History and Eschatology*, pp. 117, 118.

[15] *Ibid.*, p. 117

[16] "The Problem of Hermeneutics," pp. 253-254.

[17] *Ibid.*, p. 251.

[18] See especially the following: "New Testament and Mythologie," originally published in *Beiträge zur Evangelischen Theologie* 7 (1941), reprinted in Hans-Werner Bartsch (ed.), *Kerygma und Mythos* I (Hamburg: Reich, 1948) pp. 15-53, translated as "New Testament and Mythology" in H.W. Bartsch (ed.), *Kerygma and Myth*, I (London: S.P.C.K., 1964), pp. 1-44; "Zu Schniewinds Thesen" in *Kerygma und Mythos*, I, pp. 135-153, translated as "A Reply to the Theses of J. Schniewind" in *Kerygma and Myth*, I, pp. 102-123; "Bultmann Replies to his Critics," *op cit.*, p. 191-211; "Antwort an Karl Jaspers," in H.W. Bartsch, *Kerygma und Mythos*, III, (Hamburg: Reich, 1954), pp. 47-59, translated as "The Case for Demythologizing: A Reply" in H.W. Bartsch (ed.), *Kerygma and Myth*, II pp. 181-194; *History and Eschatology* (Edinburgh: The University Press, 1957 - first published in English); *Jesus Christ and Mythology* (New York: Charles Scribner's Sons, 1958 - first published in English; and "Zum Problem der Entmythologisiesung" in Il *Problema della Demitizzazione* (Rome: Instituto di Studi Filosofici, 1961), translated as "On the Problem of Demythologizing" in R. Batey (ed.), *New Testament Issues* (New York: Harper and Row, 1970), pp. 35-44.

[19] "New Testament and Mythology," p. 13.

[20]"The Case for Demythologizing: A Reply," p. 184.

[21]"New Testament and Mythology," p. 10. For a critical examination of Bultmann's understanding of myth, see Ronald W. Hepburn, "Demythologizing and the Problem of Validity" in A. Flew and A. MacIntyre (eds.), Karl Jaspers, "Myth and Religion" in *Kerygma and Myth*, II pp. 133-180 (*Kerygma und Mythos*, III); and Edwin M. Good, "The Meaning of Demythologization" in Charles W. Kegley (ed.), *The Theology of Rudolf Bultmann* (London: SCM, 1966), pp. 21-40.

[22]"On the Problem of Demythologizing," p. 40.

[23]"New Testament and Mythology," p. 37.

[24]*Ibid.*, p. 3.

[25]*Ibid.*, p. 15.

[26]*Ibid.*, p. 4, 5.

[27]*Ibid.*, p. 3

[28]*Ibid.*

[29]*Ibid.*, p. 4.

[30]Bultmann's own exegetical prowess is displayed in many works, including, for instance, "New Testament and Mythology," *op cit.*, pp. 17-44; *Theology of the New Testament*, vol. 1 (New York: Charles Scribner's Sons, 1951), for example, chapter II, "The Kerygma of the Earliest Church;" *Gnosis* (London: A. and C. Black, 1952); and especially *The Gospel of John* (Oxford: Basil Blackwell, 1971). The relationship between Bultmann's own exegetical practice and his hermeneutic theory is a complex one and not central to the inquiry here.

[31]"The Case for Demythologizing," p. 183.

[32] John Macquarrie, *The Scope of Demythologizing* (London: SCM Press, 1960), p. 13.

[33] Schubert M. Ogden, "Introduction" in *Existence and Faith: Shorter Writings of Rudolf Bultmann*, p. 18.

[34] "A reply to the Theses of J. Schniewind," p. 122.

[35] See "the Case for Demythologizing," p. 183 where Bultmann writes: Modern man "must be confronted with the issues of decision, be provoked to decision by the fact that the stumbling-block to faith, the skandalon, is peculiarly disturbing to man in general. ...It is by striving to clarify the meaning of faith that demythologizing leads man to the issue of decision, not by 'an intellectual assimilation of existential propositions in the Bible by means of existentialist exegesis,' nor by 'a new method for the true acquisition of faith' through existentialist interpretation."

[36] Macquarrie, *op cit.*, pp. 35-36.

[37] "New Testament and Mythology," p. 1ff.

## CHAPTER 4

## HIRSCH'S HERMENEUTICS: A CRITICAL EXAMINATION

In *Validity in Interpretation*,[1] E.D. Hirsch, Jr. agrees with Dilthey that genuine textual understanding consists of reconstruction.[2] Hirsch maintains, however, that the necessary sort of reconstruction is the reproduction on the part of the interpreter of the author's intended meaning. Hirsch argues that the author's intended meaning is what a text means,[3] and he rejects an alternate hermeneutic (which he calls "the theory of semantic autonomy") that denies this claim. The author's intended meaning represents what the interpreter is to establish if he is to interpret a text correctly. Validity in hermeneutics is grounded in this conception of textual meaning.

Hirsch points out that in current hermeneutic practice, interpretations of texts are said to be "sensitive," "rich," "interesting," "illuminating," "vital and relevant," *etc.*[4] Hirsch rejects such "aesthetic predicates" (as I shall call them) as totally inadequate for any hermeneutic whose object is accurate understanding. For one thing, two mutually incompatible interpretations of a text may be said to be "sensitive," "illuminating," *etc.* without contradiction. Similarly, even incorrect interpretations may be said to be "interesting," "rich," *etc.* Such predicates, moreover, fail to do justice to the nature of textual understanding: they simply qualify a certain sort of response or reaction to a text by an interpreter (*e.g.* what he gets out of it, sees in it, makes of it, etc.) and may have very little to do with what the text means. Most importantly, the use of such predicates ignores the necessity of having a criterion of validity, *i.e.* of having some means of judging whether or not a particular interpretation represents the correct meaning of the text. For Hirsch, this neglects the central task of hermeneutics: to establish the basis upon which interpretations can be said to be "valid."

According to Hirsch, the prevailing mode of interpretation is one which emphasizes the significance of the text for the reader, not one that stresses the meaning of the text the reader ought to grasp. This predominant hermeneutic approach Hirsch calls "the theory of semantic autonomy."[5] Very generally, the theory of semantic autonomy contends:

(a) that the author's intended meaning is irrelevant to interpretation,

(b) that having a criterion of validity for interpretation is of no importance (or, is impossible), and

(c) that aesthetic predicates suffice within criticism.[6]

According to Hirsch, this approach predominates today,[7] with disastrous consequences for hermeneutics: by eliminating from hermeneutic concern the author's intended meaning, it destroys the basis upon which interpretations can be said to be valid. This in turn vitiates the possibility of correct textual understanding, thus undermining the epistemological worth of the humanities.

This article critically examines the foundations of Hirsch's hermeneutics, looking specifically at his rejection of the theory of semantic autonomy and the arguments he advances on behalf of his own hermeneutic position. I argue that Hirsch's arguments fail to establish the author's intended meaning as the meaning of the text. Thus, although it may play some role in textual understanding, the author's intended meaning does not serve to ground hermeneutic validity.

## 1. Hirsch's Critique of The Theory of Semantic Autonomy

Hirsch contends that the theory of semantic autonomy amounts to the doctrine that "texts belong to a distinct ontological realm where meaning is independent of authorial will."[8] It is important to note that Hirsch identifies the autonomy indicated by this approach as autonomy from the author's meaning. Thus, if it can be shown that the theory of semantic autonomy is false, then not only is the nonautonomous nature of textual interpretation demonstrated, but to the extent that nonautonomous nature of textual interpretation is identical with dependency upon authorial will, then it also establishes an important foundation for supposing the approach based on the author's intended meaning as the meaning of the text is true.

The first defense of the theory of semantic autonomy (call this TSA#I) that Hirsch critically examines maintains that textual meaning changes.[9] The argument is as follows:

**TSA#I**

1. The meaning of a text changes

2. The meaning of a text changes, even for the author of the text.

   ———————————————————

   Therefore: It is pointless to take into account the author's intended meaning.

Hirsch contends that premise (1) has been widely touted in hermeneutic theory and practice. Rene Wellek and Austin Warren proclaimed it in Theory of Literature,[10] radical historicists maintained that textual meaning changes from era to era; and psychologists say that it altered from reading to reading.

Hirsch also indicates that premise (2) finds support in "the experience that everybody has when he re-reads his own work. His response to it is different."[11] Thus the argument concludes the author's meaning cannot be the object of textual interpretation. As Hirsch sees it, this would establish the autonomy of the text.

Hirsch maintains that TSA#I is fundamentally misstated and he tries to show this in three steps. His first step in rejecting TSA#I disputes the second premise for three main reasons. Hirsch's counter-argument to TSA#I is as follows (call this argument H#I):

**H#I**

> 1. There is an important distinction between revision of a text and changing textual meaning.

Hirsch acknowledges that it may be true that authors reach a point where they disagree with what they at one time had written and revise what they said accordingly. Revision of what was initially said, however, is not to change the meaning of what was originally said: it is simply to repudiate the original statement and to replace it by another statement. That textual revision occurs by authors of texts does not entail that textual meaning changes, even for the author. H#I continues:

> 2. There is an important distinction between textual meaning and an author's "response" to his text.

Hirsch notes that "the phenomenon of changing authorial responses is important because it illustrates the difference between textual meaning and what is loosely termed a 'response' to the text."[12] Arnold, for example, publicly rejected Empedocles on Etna, and Schelling rejected all his philosophical works written before 1809. But to reject what one once said is not to change the meaning of what one once said. Rather what the author once wrote is seen by him in a new light, *e.g.* as being inadequate, wrong, or muddle-headed. This sort of response by an author to his text does not entail that textual meaning changes, even for the author. Rather it simply indicates that authors may view their works subsequently in quite a different light than when they originally wrote them.

> 3. There is an important distinction between the meaning of a text and the significance of a text for someone.

He makes this distinction as follows:

> Meaning is that which is represented by a text; it is what the author meant by his use of a particular sign sequence; it is what the signs represent. Significance, on the other hand, names a relationship between that meaning and a person, or a conception, or a situation, or indeed anything imaginable. Authors, who like everyone else change their attitudes, feelings, opinions, and value criteria in the course of time, will obviously in the course of time tend to view their own work in different contexts. Clearly what changes for them is not the meaning of the work, but rather their relationship to that meaning.[13]

Thus what changes for the author is the significance the text has, not its meaning. Its meaning remains the same. Indeed it must remain the same, or else repudiation and rejection by the author of what he once wrote would be meaningless.

On the basis of premises (1), (2) and (3) of H#I above, Hirsch concludes that in TSA#I both premises (1) and (2) are false. Thus TSA#I fails to establish the autonomy of the text.

Hirsch's second step in rejecting TSA#I makes use of the distinction raised in H#I premise (3). There Hirsch drew a distinction between the meaning of a text which is unchangeable, and the significance of a text which is changeable. Hirsch contends that by failing to note this distinction, the semantic autonomists have misstated their argument. In effect they ought to be speaking about the significance of texts, not the meaning of texts. Thus the premises of TSA#I, Hirsch contends, ought to be re-written as follows:

**TSA#I**

1. The significance of a text changes.
2. The significance of a text changes, even for the author of the text.

This re-writing of the premises of TSA#I would accommodate the point made by semantic autonomists that texts can be regarded in changed circumstances in quite a different light than formerly, *e.g.* by readers in different situations and by interpreters in different cultures or generations. Hirsch does not dispute this, but argues that all this indicates is that the significance of a text may change from time to time and from person to person. This is not to say, however, that the meaning of the text changes. It remains unchangeable.

Hirsch's third step in rejection of TSA#I is a consideration of what ought to follow from TSA#I as re-written. Here Hirsch's argument is not all that clear. Certainly it does follow from TSA#I as rewritten that premises (1) and (2) of the original TSA#I are false. That much is clear, but not much follows from this one way or the other for the theory of semantic autonomy. The only conclusion that would appear to follow from the rejection of premises (1) and (2) of the original TSA#I argument would be that there is an unchangeable textual meaning.

Hirsch, however, clearly intends the argument to carry much greater weight. It ought to, and indeed does, in his estimation, say something about the relative merits of the two conflicting hermeneutic approaches. As he indicates at the end of his discussion of this particular support for the theory of semantic autonomy:

> ...enough has been said to show that the author's revaluation of his text's significance does not change its meaning and, further, that arguments which rely on such examples are not effective weapons for attacking either the stability or the normative authority of the author's original meaning.[14]

Hirsch wishes to show that semantic autonomy cannot be the case and that there is good initial support for his own hermeneutic option. A conclusion along these lines could be drawn if he were to argue as follows (call this H#II):

**H#II**

1. The significance of a text changes, and this is true even for the author of the text (from TSA#I, as re-written)

2. There is an unchangeable textual meaning for a text. (from Hirsch's rejection of TSA#I).

3. The author's intended meaning is the unchangeable textual meaning for a text.

From H#II would follow the conclusion that semantic autonomy cannot be the case.

The strength of H#II lies in Hirsch's distinction between meaning and significance, and in his contention that the meaning of a text must remain unchangeable or else the author's repudiation and rejection of what he had once written would not make sense. This contention is well-founded, and the distinction a useful one. Thus, in H#II above, premise (1) is acceptable, as is premise (2) which was derived from (1). The difficulty with the argument is premise (3), for Hirsch advances no argument to establish that the meaning of a text must be the author's intended meaning. It may very well be the case that textual meaning is unchanging without this necessarily being the unchanging author's meaning. All that Hirsch's argument establishes is that a text's meaning must be seen as unchanging so as to accommodate the intelligibility of authorial repudiation or rejection of it.

Furthermore, from the conclusion of H#II, namely that semantic autonomy cannot be the case, nothing follows in support of Hirsch's own approach. Hirsch must show that unchanging textual meaning is the unchanging author's meaning. Hirsch, however, seems to have adopted a position something like the following: if the theory of semantic autonomy cannot be the case, then the normative author's meaning approach must be true. Hirsch appears to have adopted the view that rejection of the theory of semantic autonomy is equivalent to the affirmation of the author's intended meaning approach he himself espouses. That he adopts this equivalence can be seen from his definition of the theory of semantic autonomy, as one which banishes the author from theoretical concern. This equivalence assumption might be plausible if, indeed, these hermeneutic options, and these alone, exhausted the field of available hermeneutic approaches. In which case, showing that the theory of semantic autonomy cannot be the case would establish good support in favor of the author's intended meaning approach. It would also indicate the basis upon which Hirsch can move so easily from having shown that texts have an unchangeable meaning to the view that this unchangeable meaning is the author's intended meaning (see premise (3) in H#II above). There is, however, no good reason to suppose the assumed equivalence is true. Textual meaning may be unchanging without necessarily being the unchanging author's meaning. If this is the case, then premise (3) of H#II needs considerable justification, and the relationship between a rejection of the theory of semantic autonomy and the affirmation of Hirsch's own approach needs extensive clarification.

A second defense of the theory of semantic autonomy which Hirsch examines goes as follows:[15]

**TSA#II**

> 1. The author's intended meaning is inaccessible to the interpreter (*i.e.*, it cannot be known by the interpreter).
>
> ———————————————
>
> Therefore: The author's intended meaning cannot be the object of textual interpretation.

It is important to note here that the conclusion is to be seen as support for the theory of semantic autonomy only if it is the case that Hirsch adopts the implication that if the author's intended meaning theory cannot be the case, then the approach of semantic autonomy is to be affirmed. This is additional evidence in favor of the equivalence Hirsch has been charged with having adopted.

Premise (1) of TSA#II, Hirsch notes, draws support from the following sort of observation:

> Since we are all different from the author, we cannot reproduce his intended meaning in ourselves, and even if by some accident we could, we still would not be certain that we had done so.[16]

Hirsch agrees with this observation but not with the conclusion that the semantic autonomist would wish to draw from it. His counter-argument (call it H#III) is aimed at clarifying premise (1) of TSA#II in such a way as to allow at least the partial accessibility of the author's intended meaning. In setting out his counter-argument, Hirsch observes that "since we cannot get inside the author's head, it is useless to try to reproduce a private meaning experience that cannot be reproduced."[17] Thus Hirsch contends:

**H#III**

1. Whatever is meant by "the author's intended meaning," it cannot be the private intentions known only to the author to which no interpreter could ever have access.

To this Hirsch adds that it might be reasonable to construe TSA#II as putting forth a moderate and true sceptical claim, namely:

2. "Certain texts might, because of their character or age, represent authorial meanings which are now inaccessible."[18]

Admitting this, however, is not to admit that all texts have authorial meanings which are inaccessible. TSA#II is at best true in a highly restricted sense. But perhaps this is not at all the intent of premise (1) of TSA#II. Perhaps it concerns more the degree of confidence the interpreter is entitled to have in his reconstruction or re-cognition of the author's intended meaning. Thus Hirsch maintains:

3. If premise (1) is interpreted as contending that the author's intended meaning cannot be certainly known, then it is correct.

In this case, however, it should not be concluded that the author's intended meaning is totally inaccessible and consequently an unhelpful consideration in interpretation. Hirsch grants that genuine certainty in interpretation is impossible, but also asserts that the author's meaning is at least partially accessible to the interpreter. The interpretation of texts, he points out, is concerned exclusively with shareable meanings and not with everything the author has in mind when he wrote the text. Thus, Hirsch concludes on the basis of the three premises of H#III, premise (1) of TSA#II must be modified to read that the author's meaning is at least partially accessible and therefore indispensable in textual interpretation. H#III establishes that the author's intended meaning is at least partially accessible to the interpreter.

But H#III raises two important questions. For one thing, it fails to establish the primacy of the author's intended meaning. Moreover, it seems to offer grounds for supposing that it cannot fulfill the role it is supposed to fill in Hirsch's own hermeneutics. The admission of even a moderate scepticism concerning the accessibility of the author's intended meaning, and the reliance on indirect means whereby the interpreter might have partial access to the author's intended meaning does much to vitiate its plausibility. It would appear to follow from Hirsch's admissions that different interpreters may differ on what the author's intended meaning is and it therefore cannot play the sort of decisive role that Hirsch has in mind for it. If there are many different construals of what the author's intended meaning is, then it cannot serve as the basis upon which the various construals of a text are to be judged as to validity.

Furthermore, questions are raised concerning just what "the author's intended meaning" denotes. For it would also appear to follow from Hirsch's admissions that what the author has intended to communicate via shared verbal meaning is none other than what he has communicated to the interpreter via the text. If this were the case, then the author's intended meaning would denote all and every interpretation imputed to the text. This clearly is not what Hirsch intends by "the author's intended meaning," for the latter is the meaning by means of which all imputed interpretations can be scrutinized as to correctness. How this is possible, given Hirsch's admissions, is difficult to discern.

There is, however, another source of support for the theory of semantic autonomy.[19] Hirsch introduces it as follows:

> If it can be shown (as it apparently can) that in some cases the author does not really know what he means, then it seems to follow that the author's meaning cannot constitute a general principle or norm for determining the meaning of a text, and it is precisely such a general normative principle that is required in defining the concept of validity.[20]

TSA#III goes as follows:
**TSA#III**

1. The author often does not know what he means.

   _____

   Therefore: The conclusion of TSA#III is unjustified.

For Hirsch, it is possible for the interpreter to understand the author better than he understands himself. But this sort of claim must be qualified by the distinctions he raises in premises (1), (2), and (3) of H#IV above. Kant, for instance, claimed that he understood Plato better than Plato understood himself.[21] For Hirsch, this phrasing is imprecise, "for it was not Plato's meaning that Kant understood better than Plato, but rather the subject matter that Plato was attempting to analyze."[22] It is important, therefore, to distinguish between subject matter and meaning. Similarly Hirsch acknowledges that "there are usually components of an author's intended meaning that he is not conscious of"[23] and an interpreter might make these unconscious meanings explicit, thereby claiming to understand the author better than the author understood himself. This sort of authorial ignorance is not, however, damaging to Hirsch's own hermeneutic position, for, as Hirsch maintains, an author may not understand all the implications of what he has written. Thus the normative role of the author's intended meaning is still rendered possible.

Again the difficulty lies in comprehending what constitutes the author's intended meaning, particularly if it excludes unconscious elements in the author's mind and implications derived from the author's meaning. Also what is still at stake is the basic claim itself, namely that the author's meaning is the meaning of a text and hence is the object of textual interpretation.

Finally Hirsch examines a central tenet of the theory of semantic autonomy: concern with the text, and only the text.[24] This fourth support for the theory of semantic autonomy would go as follows:

**TSA#IV**

1. It does not matter what an author means — only what his text says

   ───────────────────────────────────────

   Therefore: The theory of semantic autonomy is well-founded.

According to Hirsch, TSA#IV has been defended in a variety of ways. For one thing, T.S. Eliot in "Tradition and the Individual Talent" maintained the theory of semantic autonomy on the grounds (a) that the author has no control over the words he has loosed upon the world, and (b) that he has no special privileges as an interpreter of them.[25] Hirsch replies that if this were the case, then there would be no way of judging when a person had been misunderstood. His counter-argument to this defense of TSA#IV is as follows:

**H#V**

1. If what Eliot says is true, then the theory of textual interpretation would offer no criterion of validity.

2. But a theory of interpretation ought to offer a criterion of validity.

---

Therefore: Eliot's account is to be rejected.

By 'validity' Hirsch indicates that he means "the correspondence of an interpretation to a meaning which is represented by the text."[26] In support of premise (1) of H#V, Hirsch contends that if the text and only the text were the object of textual interpretation, then there would be no way of adjudicating different interpretations of the text: the text can say different things to different readers. But presumably the author meant something by the text, Hirsch asserts, and it is not unreasonable to expect interpreters to discover what he meant.

TSA#IV has been defended in a different way, Hirsch points out, by Wimsatt and Beardsley in "The Intentional Fallacy,"[27] who present the following argument:

> The author's desire to communicate a particular meaning is not necessarily the same as his success in doing so. Since his actual performance is presented in his text, any special attempt to divine his intention would falsely equate his private wish with his public accomplishment.[28]

Consequently the theory of textual interpretation must distinguish between the author's intentions (which are irrelevant) and the author's accomplishment

# Hirsch's Hermeneutics: A Critical Examination

(namely, the text itself), and must focus on the latter as the object of interpretation.

Hirsch's counter-argument is essentially along the lines of the response he offered to T.S. Eliot in H#V, namely that if this account were true, then no criterion of validity would be possible. "If a text means what it says, then it means nothing in particular."[29] On this account, the meaning of a text would simply be what its readers happen to construe it to mean without there being any way to evaluate their construals.

Hirsch's counter-argument here at best amounts to an assertion that there ought to be a criterion of validity of interpretations of texts. It in no way establishes the content of that criterion. Nor does it advance the argument that such a criterion is both necessary and possible. Furthermore, H#V does little to demolish the contention of the semantic autonomists that the text represents the author's achievement and that it constitutes the primary object of textual interpretation. Nor does H#V in itself rule out the possibility of different sorts of criteria of validity, one compatible with the theory of semantic autonomy. One such criterion might be: that of several interpretations of the same text, the best reading is the one which does greatest justice to the text taken as a whole.

## 2. Critical Assessment of Hirsch's Position

In Hirsch's estimation, the alternative to the theory of semantic autonomy is the reinstatement of the author's meaning as normative and the recognition of the importance of re-cognitive reconstruction on the part of the interpreter of the author's outlook. In Hirsch's own approach to hermeneutics, there are two fundamental claims: (1) that the text's meaning is the author's intended meaning, and (2) that the author's meaning provides a criterion (for Hirsch, the only criterion) by means of which the validity of interpretations can be judged.

There are several conceivable roles within hermeneutics that the author's intended meaning could play, and it is important to note exactly what Hirsch is claiming. In textual interpretation generally, it surely is important to note what an author is trying to do, what problem he is addressing, what approach he has adopted and for what reasons, and what he hopes his text will accomplish. Often in a preface or introduction the author will set before the reader the context within which he hopes his text will be read. In this case, the author's intended meaning would be authoritative for textual interpretation, *i.e.*, it would represent an aspect of textual interpretation which the conscientious interpreter ought to take into account in order to give the text an accurate "valid" reading.

One claim, then, that can be made about the role of the author's intended meaning in textual interpretation is this: (a) that appeal to the author's intended meaning is an important, even indispensable, aid in textual interpretation. This claim draws its support from interpretive practice, and it would allow that there may be other important, even indispensable, aids involved in textual interpretation. Moreover, claim (a) does not bind the interpreter to what the author intends. That is, the interpreter may take into account the author's intended meaning, be aware of it, have considered it, and yet finally reject it. Even rejection of the author's intended meaning by the interpreter after due consideration would be compatible with the role ascribed on claim (a) to the author's intended meaning.

Claim (a) is not Hirsch's claim about the role of the author's intended meaning. Hirsch's claim is this: (b) that the meaning of the text (*i.e.*, the one correct meaning which the interpreter ought to grasp) is the author's intended meaning. Hirsch's claim is one of identity between the text's meaning and the author's meaning. In terms of claim (b), the author's intended meaning is not only authoritative for textual interpretation: it is identical with it. It constitutes the object of interpretation; it is that for which the interpreter searches in his quest for a "valid" interpretation of a text. That Hirsch makes claim (b) and not claim (a) is seen directly from statements he makes (*e.g.*, "...a text means what its author meant.")[30] and from the compatibility of claim (a) with multiple acceptable interpretations of a text which claim (b) would rule out.

If claim (b) is what Hirsch intends, then what does "the author's intended meaning" denote? For one thing, "the author's intended meaning" cannot mean what the author intended to mean but did not succeed in meaning, for then the author's meaning would not be normative for textual interpretation in the way Hirsch wishes it to be. Furthermore, it cannot mean what the author intended to accomplish by having written the work *i.e.*, what he hoped to achieve by writing the work, *e.g.*, to inform, titillate, shock, annoy, *etc.* the reader. Nor can it mean the author's own personal meaning experiences. Such experiences are irreproducible, and the irreproducibility of the author's private experiences would entail the irreproducibility of meaning, a consequent which for Hirsch is false.[31] Nor does "the author's intended meaning" denote all the meanings the author entertained when he wrote the text, for the meanings an author can convey are perhaps more limited than the meanings he can entertain.

In "Objective Interpretation," Hirsch points out that for Husserl, different intentional acts (on different occasions) "intend" an identical intentional object.[32] The example Hirsch uses is the following:

> ... when I "intend" a box, there are at least three distinguishable aspects of that event. First, there is the object as perceived by me; second, there is the act by which I perceive the object; and finally, there is (for physical things) the object which exists independently of my perceptual act. The first two aspects of the event Husserl calls "intentional object" and "intentional act" respectively.[33]

As applied to textual interpretation, Hirsch's point is that while the reader and author are different, and while their psychological acts differ, they may yet intend the same intentional object, viz., the meaning of the text. As Hirsch points out, the author's intended meaning is a shareable verbal meaning.[34] Verbal meaning is, for Hirsch, unchanging. It has been permanently fixed in the text by the author. While reproducible by different intentional acts, it remains self-identical throughout all the reproductions.[35]

Thus, for Hirsch, the author's intended meaning is the meaning he has given the text. It is not an ancillary datum for interpretation to be taken under consideration at the interpreter's discretion: it constitutes, rather, the principal object of interpretation. Hirsch is quite clear that he is asserting claim (b). On occasion, however, it must be admitted that Hirsch speaks as though claim (a) were the case. For instance, Hirsch says that:

> ...hermeneutics must stress a reconstruction of the author's aims and attitudes in order to evolve guides and norms for construing the meaning of his text.[36]

From this it might be inferred that the interpreter takes the author's aims and attitudes into account in order to do something further, namely to give an interpretation to the text. But this is not faithful to Hirsch's over-all intentions, for if claim (a) were the case, then the author's meaning would not serve as a normative principle enabling the interpreter to select from an array of interpretive possibilities the one and only meaning the text must have. Claim (b) is Hirsch's contention.

Hirsch tries to safeguard claim (b) from two possible misinterpretations. On the one hand, the author's intended meaning is not the text itself. Rather what the author intends is the meaning of the text and it is this which properly constitutes the interpretive object. On the other hand, the author's intended

# Hirsch's Hermeneutics: A Critical Examination

meaning is not to be sought outside of the text, as if it were to be located within the author himself. On the contrary, it is embedded in the text itself.

That the text's meaning is the author's intended meaning and that it serves as the criterion for interpretive validity is defended by Hirsch in several ways. On the one hand, he has tried to show the theory of semantic autonomy cannot be the case, thereby not only clearing the way for his own approach but also actually lending it considerable support. But to show that semantic autonomy is not the case, unless it is supposed that one approach is equivalent to the other's negation, or equivalently, that the two approaches are mutually exclusive and mutually exhaust the range of hermeneutic options. Thus one argument Hirsch appears to use is the following (call it H1):

**H1**

1. Either the theory of semantic autonomy or (exclusive sense of 'or') the author's intended meaning approach is true. (Hirsch's equivalence assumption)

2. The theory of semantic autonomy is false. (see arguments examined in section 1 above)

   ---

   Therefore: The author's intended meaning approach is true.[37]

Closely associated with this argument is another:

**H2**

1. Either the theory of semantic autonomy or (exclusive sense) the author's intended meaning approach is true.

2. If the theory of semantic autonomy were the case, then texts would not have determinate interpretations (*i.e.*, texts would not be capable of having one and only one correct interpretation).[38]

3. If textual interpretation is to occur, then texts must have determinate interpretations.

4. Texts do have determinate interpretations.

---

Therefore: The theory of semantic autonomy cannot be the case. (And, by virtue of premise 1, thus the author's intended meaning approach must be the case).[39]

Both H1 and H2 rely heavily on the equivalence assumption in premise (1). But also of crucial importance is premise (4) in H2, for without it, the argument would fail to be valid. Generally Hirsch simply makes claim (3) and he insists on this over and over again. He recognizes he "will have to show that the author's verbal meaning is determinate, that it is reproducible."[40] He does this by contending that verbal meaning must be both "a willed type" (Chapter Two) and "a shared type" (Chapter Three). His notion of a willed type is as follows:

> ...verbal meaning can be defined as a willed type which an author expresses by linguistic symbols and which can be understood by another through those symbols.[41]

Verbal meaning as shared type is simply the other side:

> If verbal meaning is a willed type that can be conveyed through linguistic signs, it follows that the possibility of

# Hirsch's Hermeneutics: A Critical Examination 107

> conveying the willed type depends on the interpreter's prior experience of the willed type. Otherwise, the interpreter could not generate implications; he would not know which implications belonged to the meaning and which did not. The willed type must be shared type in order for communication to occur.[42]

This, however, does not establish that communication or the shareability of verbal meaning occurs, much less does it demonstrate that texts have determinate interpretations. Rather it is to contend either that texts ought to have determinate interpretations or can have determinate interpretations if communicability and meaning are seen as willed and shared types. In effect, this supports premise (3) by contending, in other words, that if textual interpretation is to occur, the meaning must be viewed as a sharing of the author's meaning. It in no way demonstrates the truth of premise (4), namely that texts do have determinate interpretations. Without support for premise (4), argument H2 fails.

In a somewhat different vein, Hirsch offers this argument:

**H3**

1. There are no meanings outside of persons who mean.[43]

2. In textual interpretation, meaning can be either the interpreter's or (exclusive sense) the author's.

3. Meaning cannot be just the interpreter's meaning.

> Therefore: Textual meaning must be the author's intended meaning.

The reason for premise (3) has again to do with determinateness of textual interpretation. If meaning were simply what the interpreter makes out of the text, then there could be no basis upon which the determinateness of interpretations could be established.

Finally, Hirsch notes that the distinction between meaning and significance necessitates a further distinction between the theory of textual interpretation (having to do with meaning) and criticism (having to do with significance). Hirsch charges the theory of semantic autonomy with having confused significance with meaning and therefore offering as theory of interpretation what properly is an account of criticism. By making the distinction between meaning and significance, Hirsch claims that his own hermeneutic approach avoids the conflation of interpretation with criticism and thereby all the confusion this assimilation engenders.

Hirsch's defense of the author's intended meaning as the meaning of the text poses many important problems that would appear to undermine his own position. For one thing, interpreters may differ concerning the reconstruction of the author's intended meaning. This may be the case in interpretive practice where interpreters honestly and sincerely try to ascertain what the author may have or must have meant when he wrote a text. What the author intended is not at all that transparent. It is not as if the author's intended meaning *per se* stood outside of the interpretations of the author's intended meaning of which there may be many.

From this it follows that the author's intended meaning cannot serve in a constitutive fashion as the meaning of the text. All that are available are differing construals by the interpreters involved concerning what the author may have meant. It is not a matter of one interpreter having it (*i.e.*, the author's intended meaning) and the other interpreters failing to have it. This hermeneutic approach fails to establish a basis upon which the meaning of the text becomes apparent.

It also follows that the author's intended meaning cannot serve the normative role ascribed to it by Hirsch. A new array of interpretive possibilities is presented, namely different interpreters' judgments concerning what the author may have or must have meant. There is no independently establishable meaning which is ascertainable that adjudicates the competing assessments of what the author may have or must have meant. Thus this hermeneutic approach fails to provide a basis upon which one and only one interpretation may be selected.

From Hirsch's account, he seems to think that there is one and only one interpreted author's intended meaning, and to suppose so simply represents the quest for the elusive interpretive Holy Grail, *viz.*, the positing beyond the realm of interpretation that by means of which interpretations themselves can be judged.

## ENDNOTES

[1] E.D. Hirsch, Jr., *Validity in Interpretation* (New Haven: Yale University Press, 1967). See also his two earlier essays, "Objective Interpretation," *Proceedings of the Modern Language Association* 75 (1960), 463-479 [reprinted as Appendix I of *Validity in Interpretation*] and "Truth and Method in Interpretation," *The Review of Metaphysics* 18 (1965), 488-507 [reprinted as Appendix II of *Validity in Interpretation*] as well as his more recent book, *The Aims of Interpretation* (Chicago: University of Chicago Press, 1976). In this latter work Hirsch claims that "these essays do not, in any respect that I am aware of, represent substantive revisions of the earlier argument" (p. 7). Without evaluating this claim, this examination of Hirsch's hermeneutics will focus on his treatment in *Validity in Interpretation*.

[2] As Hirsch says, "The interpreter's primary task is to reproduce in himself the author's 'logic,' his attitudes, his cultural givens, in short, his world ...the ultimate verificative principle is very simple — the imaginative reconstruction of the speaking subject." *Validity in Interpretation*, Appendix I, p. 242.

[3] *Ibid.*, pp. 1, 25, and Appendix I, p. 235.

[4] *Ibid.*, p. 10, and Appendix I, p. 235.

[5] *Ibid.*, pp. viii, l, 4.

[6] *Ibid.*, Chapter One.

[7] Hirsch points out that "... there has been in the past four decades a heavy and largely victorious assault on the sensible belief that a text means what its author meant. In the earliest and most decisive wave of the attach (launched by Eliot, Pound, and their associates) the battle-ground was literary: the proposition that textual meaning is independent of the author's control was associated with the literary doctrine that the best poetry is impersonal, objective, and autonomous; that it leads an afterlife of its own, totally cut off from the life of its author." *Ibid.*, p. 1. Other semantic autonomists include, according to Hirsch, M.K. Wimsatt, M.C. Beardsley, Heidegger, Bultmann and Gadamer.

[8] *Ibid.* p. viii.

[9]*Ibid.*, pp. 6-10.

[10]Rene Wellek and Austin Warren, *Theory of Literature* (New York: Harcourt, Brace and Co., 1956).

[11]Hirsch, *Validity in Interpretation*, p. 7.

[12]*Ibid.*

[13]*Ibid.*, p. 8. See also Appendix I, pp. 210ff., and pp. 214ff.

[14]*Ibid.*, p. 10.

[15]*Ibid.*, pp. 14-19.

[16]*Ibid.*, p. 14.

[17]*Ibid.*, p. 16.

[18]*Ibid.*, pp. 18, 19.

[19]*Ibid.*, pp. 19-23.

[20]*Ibid.*, p. 20,

[21]The reference here is to Immanuel Kant, *Critique of Pure Reason* trans. Norman Kemp Smith (London: MacMillan and Co., 1958), A 314, B 370, p. 310: "I shall not engage here in any literary enquiry into the meaning which this illustrious philosopher [Plato] attached to the expression. I need only remark that it is by no means unusual, upon comparing the thoughts which an author has expressed in regard to his subject, whether in ordinary conversation or in writing, to find that we understand him better than he has understood himself."

[22]Hirsch, *op cit.*, p. 20.

[23]*Ibid.*, p. 21.

[24]*Ibid.*, pp. 10-14.

[25]See T.S. Eliot, "Tradition and the Individual Talent," in *The Sacred Wood* (London: Methuen, 1960).

[26]Hirsch, *op. cit.*, p. 10.

[27]W.K. Wimsatt and Monroe C. Beardsley, "The Intentional Fallacy," *Sewanee Review* 54 (1946), and reprinted in W.K. Wimsatt, *The Verbal Icon* (Lexington, Ky.: The University of Kentucky Press, 1954), ch. 1.

[28]Hirsch, *op cit.*, p. 11.

[29]*Ibid.*, p. 13.

[30]*Ibid.*, p. 1.

[31]*Ibid.*, p. 16 and pp. 31-40.

[32]*Ibid.*, Appendix I, p. 218.

[33]*Ibid.*

[34]Note what Hirsch says about verbal meaning: "Verbal meaning is simply a special kind of intentional object, and like any other one, it remains self-identical over against the many different acts which 'intend' it. But the noteworthy feature of verbal meaning is its supra-personal character. It is not an intentional object for simply one person, but for many — potentially for all persons. Verbal meaning is, by definition, that aspect of a speaker's 'intention' which, under linguistic conventions, may be shared by others." *Ibid.*, p. 218. (Italics in the original)

[35]*Ibid.*, Appendix I, p. 219.

[36]*Ibid.*, Appendix I, p. 224.

[37]Reconstructed from *Validity in Interpretation*, Chapter One.

[38]Hirsch says, "To say that verbal meaning is determinate is not to exclude complexities of meaning but only to insist that a text's meaning is what it is and not a hundred other things." *Ibid.*, Appendix I, p. 230. Furthermore, after pointing out that determinancy is a necessary condition for validity (p. 11) and that it is a minimum requirement for share ability (p. 45), Hirsch states, "Verbal meaning, then, is what it is and not something else, and it is always the same. That is what I mean by determinancy." *Ibid.*, p. 46.

[39]Reconstructed from *Validity in Interpretation*, Chapters One and Two.

[40]*Ibid.*, p. 27.

[41]*Ibid.*, p. 49.

[42]*Ibid.*, p. 66.

[43]Hirsch states, "meaning requires a meaner." *Ibid.*, Appendix I, p. 234. He also points out that "there is no magic land of meanings outside human consciousness." *Ibid.*, p. 4.

# PART THREE:

# HERMENEUTIC STUDIES

# CHAPTER 5

# PLATO: SOME INCONSISTENCIES

## 1. The Harmonizing View

Some scholars have noted Plato's inconsistencies, Grote, Woozley and Ryle[1] among them, and have sought to account for these anomalies of reasoning. There have been inconsistencies noted between *The Apology* and *Crito*, and attempts have been made to account for these on the basis of deliberateness for a purpose (Grote)[2], or unwittingly, or because the inconsistency is only apparent (Woozley).

There are other instances of inconsistency: for example, between *The Republic* and *The Apology*, as I shall subsequently show. And there are discrepancies between the widely held view that in his dialogues, Plato has a philosophy which he is propounding versus Plato's own insistence in *Epistle VII* that he has not written down his philosophy.[3]

These inconsistencies fly in the face of a persistent tendency in Plato scholarship to present Plato's philosophy as "all of a piece," perhaps contrasting early versus later philosophy, or by showing some development.[4] On this approach, however, there appears to be the assumption that Plato is the presenter of a philosophy that he is expressing in and through his dialogues, and that the purpose of his writing is to articulate a philosophical point of view. This "harmonizing" view of Plato is reminiscent of biblical scholarship several centuries ago — to view the corpus of dialogues as one text, and not to note discrepancies, the shifts in genre, nor to relate the text to the circumstances of its having been written, *i.e.* to its Sitz-im-Leben.

This paper explores some of the curious discrepancies in Plato's thought. I shall argue that Plato's inconsistencies are real, deliberate, and done for a purpose — not the purpose suggested by Grote but for another. Also, while Plato undoubtedly has a philosophy which he expresses through his dialogues, I shall contend that the presentation of his philosophy is incidental to his primary purpose.

## 2. The Crito versus Apology

There are four major discrepancies between *Crito* and *The Apology*.[5]

First of all, in *The Apology*, Socrates has an overriding sense of mission. After stating what the accusations are, denying that he charged fees, he then examines how the slanders against him have originated. It is in this context that he appeals to his sense of mission as being the reason why he does what he does and will continue to do so. In so doing, he makes certain "mission-claims:"

> M1. He continues the investigation the gods bade him to carry out, seeking out anyone whom he thinks is wise. If not, Socrates comes to the assistance of the god and shows him he is not wise. (23b)
>
> M2. He refers to this as his service to the god. (23b)
>
> M3. He states he will obey the god rather than the jury about not practising philosophy if granted a conditional discharge. (29d)
>
> M4. He stresses there is no greater blessing for the city than his service to the god (30a): he is god's gift, a gadfly.

> M5. He claims he is led by a voice (a divine sign from the god) which steers him away from certain courses of action.(31d)

These five mission-claims cover different areas. M1 stresses the origin of his activity — continuing the investigation with which he had been charged. His methodology grows out of his sense of mission. M2 stresses the character of the mission, while M3 emphasizes its ultimacy or at the very least its higher order priority over the claims of a jury decision which conflicts with what he perceives as his mandate. M4 cites the social benefits, although in what way his activity provides a benefit to the city is not indicated in any detail. M5 points out its curious impact on Socrates which, while not indicating a positive course of action, rules out other ones.

In *Crito*, there is no sense of mission, and no mission-claims are expressed. This is curious. This is not to be accounted for because the mission is virtually over, the resigned-to-his-fate portrait in Xenophon's Apology.[6] Rather in both Apology and *Crito*, Socrates is presented as resolute, in command, and decisive. In both cases, he takes a stand. The difference lies that whereas in *The Apology* Socrates resolves the issues by appealing to his mission, in the *Crito* there is no mention of this fundamental conviction.

Secondly, in *The Apology*, there is a methodology set forward. It is in part exemplified in the report that the god has said to Chairephon that Socrates was the wisest of people. Socrates refuses to accept that at face value and engages in a pattern of activity that became his hallmark. He is perplexed. He investigates. And, after having clarified the meaning of this remark, he concludes.

In *Crito*, while Socrates questions, he does so in an intriguingly different way than in *The Apology*. After the emphasis on questioning in *The Apology*, one would expect that in *Crito*, Socrates would ask, should one always obey the law?

Or, ought one to obey a law that is unjust? Indeed, the whole treatise would then focus on the putative normative role of law. Rather, he proceeds, without questioning, to supply an answer, and contends that one ought always to obey the law, citing here the analogy with socialization within society. In the light of *The Apology*, this approach is quite unexpected, and uncharacteristic.

This, too, is curious. Why is his methodology so differently applied? And why is the question the reader is longing to hear Socrates ask, not asked? Indeed, why does the *Crito* have all the appearance of a rationalization, with the conclusion foregone and all the reasons an after-the-fact camouflage?

Thirdly, in *The Apology*, Socrates cites obedience to the god as ultimate (M3), and certainly as more authoritative than a jury decision. M3 indicates that he is prepared to disregard any jury decision that would attempt to prevent him from the exercise of philosophy. M3 is only one indication of a contemptuous and obstinate attitude that pervades *The Apology*. Socrates is defiant, and is so on the basis of an overriding conviction: obedience to the god takes precedence over social arrangements.

This appeal to an overriding consideration, based upon an alleged historic encounter of Chairephon with the Oracle, represents a curious stand, especially for a rigorous questioner. Moreover, in the light of the social circumstances of the times, it is also somewhat perplexing. Is Socrates taking a stand on the intellectual battle of the time, between the new humanism (expressed in the thinking of the atomists, Protagoras, the new art and medicine) versus the old Olympian religion with its rites and rituals? Or is he striking out in a different direction, sure to anger both sides in this debate?

In *Crito*, however, the law is absolute, whether just or unjust, and whether unjustly applied. Socrates does not raise the question, should only just laws be obeyed (as part of one's societal obligations)? Nor does he attempt to set up an overriding provision above the law (e.g. the gods) by means of which laws could be judged just or unjust. Rather Socrates appears to hold the following view:

> C1. One ought always to obey the law.

In the light of the disregard Socrates is prepared to show the jury in *The Apology*, Socrates' insistence in *Crito* on the power of law is remarkable. How does C1 relate to M3?

There are, however, some indications that Socrates' own views may not be totally consistent on this view, for alongside mission-claims in *The Apology*, Socrates also expresses some fundamental principles. These include:

> P1. A person should look only to this in his actions, whether what he does is right or wrong. (28b)
>
> P2. Do not fear death. (40c-41b)
>
> P3. The unexamined life is not worth living for man. (38a)

Principle P3 would be consistent with mission-claims M1 and M4, for the outgrowth of investigating is questioning and examining of positions, and this, probably, would be one of the blessings for the city that his activity provides.

How looking to what is right or wrong (P1) relates to obeying the god (M3) is not entirely clear. But whatever the outcome of that discussion, how C1 relates to either M3 or P1 is not clear either. In terms of obeying the god, looking to what is right or wrong, and obeying the law, what takes priority?

Fourthly, Socrates in *The Apology* dispenses with the opinions of the multitude and encourages his listeners to heed only the one who knows, the expert. Similarly, in *Crito*, he makes the same plea. But what he says, and what he accomplishes are two different things, for in *Crito*, by acquiescing in his punishment, he obeys the voice of the multitude, the jury. Rather than by inquiring into what the one who knows would do and say about the situation, he closes discussion with claim C1.

In sum the portrait of Socrates that emerges in *Crito* differs considerably from that depicted in *The Apology*: that to which Socrates appeals differs, and his methodology is not similarly applied. There is, in *Crito*, only the semblance of questioning: here Socrates has the answers which he defends without much examination.

## 3. Inconsistencies within The Republic

There are curious inconsistencies, too, within *The Republic*, although this has often been read as a straightforward proposal for an ideal just society. And, indeed, there are inconsistencies between *The Republic* and *The Apology*.

Structurally, apart from a rather lengthy setup in Book I, *The Republic* divides into three main parts. The first part represents the implementation phase of the proposal, how Plato would propose putting his ideal society in place. As we learn, it would require two major modifications: a change in the educational structure, and a change in the political structure. The second part concerns the objectives ("the four virtues") of his proposed society: to create a wise, courageous, just and temperate society. The third part concerns the rationale for the proposal, and, with some digressions, focuses on three main lines of reasoning: because of the nature of human nature, because of the nature of knowledge, and because of the nature of the afterlife.[7]

It should be noted that the order in which Plato presents his proposal is curious, for it does not correspond with the modern order for proposal writing: to state objectives first, then develop means of implementation, and state rationale. Plato takes his readers through implementation matters first, then objectives, then rationale, an order that often creates difficulties for contemporary students coming to *The Republic* for the first time. By the time they have finished the educational reform sections, they have already formed a well-established repugnant impression of what *The Republic* is proposing.

Nor is there any fourth section, whereby the objectives would be used to evaluate the suggested means of implementation. For example, a contemporary proposal writer or critic would assess the proposed means of implementation against the stated objectives. Indeed, the author of a contemporary proposal would be expected to have considered various alternative means of arriving at the stated objectives and to have evaluated them critically before settling upon one recommended course of action.

There are problems, however, with Plato's proposal. In the first place, there are serious discrepancies between the first part of the proposal and the second. In terms of the means of implementation, while there is class mobility, the discussion suggests rigidity and inflexibility. Plato's educational system is aimed at character formation, in keeping with the desirable pattern of the healthy personality in which reason is dominant, the spirited part assists reason, and the irrational part is kept in check. Literature, drama and music are to be carefully "selected," (to avoid Cornford's question-begging term 'censored.') to reinforce character traits Plato deems worthwhile. While these include accepting responsibility for one's own actions and not blaming the gods, the failure to expose students to a variety of views and lifestyles can seem highly restrictive. The political structure, while emphasizing that ruling is a specialty requiring its own skills and knowledge, seems (at least to most modern audiences) excessively repressive.

The impression one can legitimately gain from the first part of *The Republic* is that of a restrictive, rigid society where people conform to "the Truth."

In terms of objectives, however, the four virtues, there is greater room for flexibility. According to Plato, his proposed society should exhibit four characteristics: wisdom, courage, justice, and temperance. Wisdom, expressed in society through the rulers (the executive managers), could include questioning, decision-making, and an ability to change situations creatively in the light of new knowledge. Courage could include the fortitude to make the required changes, as expressed through the Guardian or administrative body. And justice, as Plato describes it, does seem to include individual fulfilment within the context of a fulfilling society. Temperance would be a virtue required by all, for it would represent the foundation upon which society would foster and encourage a tolerance for others with differing aptitudes and abilities — indeed tolerance would be essential for such a society to function effectively.

This might argue for a somewhat more open society than the initial segment of *The Republic* would suggest.

The line of interpretation that views *The Republic* as articulating the roots of totalitarianism finds support in passages in which I have described above as section one. The opposing lines of interpretation that find *The Republic* fostering or at least striving towards a more democratic or liberating society finds support in section two.8 In sum, the two differing sections of *The Republic* lead the interpreter in different interpretive directions.

If the proposal were being presented in a modern context, whereby objectives are used to assess and evaluate means of implementation, we would question whether these changes would achieve the desired objectives. And, indeed, whether they are the only possible means to achieve Plato's stated objectives. On the face of it, with these means of implementation, Plato's objectives seem highly unlikely to materialize. Stated more bluntly, Plato is faced with a dilemma. If he is serious about his means of implementation, then his objectives are unlikely to be achieved; if, on the other hand, he is serious about his objectives, then these means of implementation are unlikely to bring these about.

Secondly, there is, along the way, a curious set of omissions. For example, there is remarkably no emphasis in his proposed educational reforms on questioning, and learning how to question, the very thing for which Socrates was famous. On the conventional view, Plato was in awe of Socrates, and, if so, then it is truly perplexing that Plato's educational system would not in essence be a school for questioning. In this sense, Plato's Republic is considerably at odds with Socrates as portrayed in *The Apology*.

Moreover, there is no criticism of the pedagogical system. Like many other things in *The Republic*, it seems "fixed," forever, without change or mechanisms for change, a Parmenidean permanence. The discussion does not proceed, should the educational or political structure be shaped in this or that way to achieve certain objectives. Rather the discussion presents a fait accompli: society must be fashioned in this or that way. It is not in any sense exploratory, nor does it use questioning to uncover and critically examine the alternatives. In this way *The Republic* is closer to *Crito* in defending an affirmation than the investigatory Apology.

There is, additionally, no stress on imagination or creativity. There is none of the tremendous artistic and creative sense for which Plato himself was noted in designing and composing his dialogues. It is indeed ironic that the rich artistic genre — dialogue, story, myth, allegory — in which the proposal is itself presented would not itself be the result of the curriculum propounded by *The Republic*.

Even later on, in the "Cave" approach to education for the rulers, there is little explicit emphasis there on questioning, criticism, or imaginative pursuits. Rather the emphasis is on the solitary nature of the pursuit towards Truth, its difficulty and its alienating effect on the pursuer of Truth.

In sum, then, the proposal lacks internal consistency. In an interdialogue context, moreover, *The Republic* seems at variance with *The Apology*. Nowhere is there an emphasis on the kind of questioning exhibited by Socrates.

## 4. Why Dialogues?

Plato presents us, then, with several important enigmas that require hermeneutic explanation. How should these works be interpreted?

First let us examine *The Republic* and here there are several options. The standard view is that the dialogue is a straightforward proposal: this is the sort of ideal society Plato would wish to see. On this line of interpretation, Plato is proposing major changes in the political and educational structure of society and is advocating specialized education for the rulers of society. This line of interpretation, however, presents problems of coherence (the objectives versus the means of implementation) and problems of omission (*e.g.* training in questioning skills).

It could also be interpreted as a spoof on Sparta, with the implication that such a society should be rejected. The difficulty with such a view is that there is no direct evidence that the dialogue is entirely ironic. The genre seems entirely straightforward in tone and manner.

Thirdly, it could be that Plato is attempting something quite different in writing *The Republic*, namely, that he is presenting his hearers/readers with a discussion designed to elicit their views on the nature of the ideal society. This view treats the reader/hearer of *The Republic* as an active participant in the discussion, and not just as a passive observer of the interaction between Socrates and his companions. Seen in this light, the dialogue as a whole raises the question, how, then, should society be structured? Should it be along the lines suggested? Rather than being the end result of Plato's proposal, the dialogue, as such, represents the beginning stages of inquiry. Indeed, it represents a vehicle for inquiry to be brought to light, through the discussion of all the parties involved, including the reader/hearer.

Drew Hyland draws attention to the philosophical significance of the dialogical form:

> The Platonic dialogue does not enable us to "forget to philosophize" by dwelling endlessly on textual subtleties because the very function of the dialogue, manifested

> most clearly in the "aporia" dialogues, is to drive the reader beyond the dialogue itself....We must go beyond the dialogue because it forces us to do so.[9]

Hyland tries to reconcile Plato's dialogues with Plato's claim that he never wrote his philosophy by citing the never-ending nature of the dialogical form. Many of Plato's dialogues end with an urging that the conversation be continued at a later date, and, by implication, by us, the reader/hearer, as well. His dialogues, then, are imitations of philosophy, not philosophy per se and in this sense, Hyland suggests, Plato never did write down his philosophy.

Hyland concludes that:

> With such a framework [i.e. this view of dialogues] we may begin to glimpse in the challenges of the dialogue as a whole the far greater and more precarious challenge of which it is the imitation, and to which it is an invitation.[10]

The view that the dialogue form is invitational to philosophy is a suggestive one. I think, however, that the claim can be expressed in much stronger terms. To accomplish this, I wish to suggest that Plato's dialogues represent a distinctive genre, much in the same way that it has become appreciated in biblical scholarship since Julicher that the parables of Jesus represent a distinctive genre. Since this appreciation, biblical scholarship has attempted to provide a line of interpretation of the parables that has come to replace the older view that they represent allegories.[11]

I suggest that the dialogues be viewed as provocations, as prods to thought. The flow of conversation exemplified in the dialogue serves, on this line of interpretation, to goad the participants, including the reader/hearer, into thought on the topic at hand. They become participants in the conversation.

This view has several consequences. First of all, Plato's position is not then all that clear. Nowhere does Plato write in the first person, and there is no good reason to suppose that his view is the same as that expressed by Socrates in the dialogues. Rather Plato's purpose is fulfilled in designing and writing the dialogues so as to elicit philosophical thinking from those who encounter the dialogues.

Secondly, the loose ends in the dialogues, including the inconsistencies and the discrepancies noted here, let alone the flaws in logic noted by others, matter less when the dialogues are viewed as provocations to further reflection. Indeed, the inconsistencies and discrepancies would help provoke the reader/hearer into reflection, driving him to sort out the confusions and hopefully to achieve clarification. In this sense the inconsistencies and discrepancies do not constitute a philosophic failure, but fulfill a philosophic objective: to drive people to critical thinking.

Finally, *The Republic*, while it fails to provide a school for questioning, becomes itself a masterpiece of questioning, provoking the participants in the discussion into deeper and more sustained reflection on the nature of a better society, the purpose of education, and human destiny.

## ENDNOTES

[1] See George Grote, *Plato, and the Other Companions of Socrates* (London: John Murray, 1885); A.D. Woozley, *Law and Obedience: The Arguments of Plato's Crito* (London: Duckworth, 1979); and Gilbert Ryle, *Plato's Progress* (Cambridge: The University Press, 1966).

[2] "The dialogue called Kriton is, in one point of view, a second part or sequel — in another point of view, an antithesis or corrective — of the Platonic Apology." Grote, *op.cit.*, p. 425.

[3] Glenn R. Morrow (trans.), *Plato's Epistles* (Indianapolis: Bobbs-Merrill, 1962). "There is no writing of Plato's, nor will there ever be..." (314c) Note, too, Phaedrus 275-279 where Plato expresses reservations about the merits of writing down one's ideas.

[4] See, for instance, the many books entitled "Plato's Philosophy of ..." or "Plato's Early Philosophy of ..." or "Plato's Later Philosophy of ...".

[5] For the most part I have used G.M.A. Grube's translation, *The Trial and Death of Socrates* (Indianapolis: Hackett, 1975) while consulting T.G. and G.S. West's, *Four Texts on Socrates* (Ithaca: Cornell University Press, 1984) and Harold North Fowler, *Plato*, I (London: Heinemann, 1914, reprinted 1960).

[6] Xenophon, *Recollections of Socrates and Socrates Defense Before the Jury*, trans. Anna S. Benjamin (Indianapolis: Bobbs-Merrill, 1965).

[7] What I call "section one" extends from Book II 357a - IV 427c; "section two" extends from Book IV 427c - 434d; and "section three," Book IV 434d - end of Book X.

[8] See articles included in Thomas Thorson (ed.), *Plato: Totalitarian or Democrat?* (Englewood Cliffs: Prentice-Hall, 1963).

[9] Drew Hyland, "Why Plato Wrote Dialogues," *Philosophy and Rhetoric* 1 (1968), p.40.

[10] Hyland, *op.cit.*, p. 49.

[11]See, for instance, works such as Norman Perrin, *Jesus and the Language of the Kingdom* (Philadelphia: Fortress Press, 1976) or Dan Otto Via, Jr., *The Parables* (Philadelphia: Fortress Press, 1967).

## Also Consulted

Harold Cherniss, *The Riddle of the Ancient Academy* (Berkeley: University of California Press, 1945).

Thomas G. West, *Plato's Apology of Socrates* (Ithaca: Cornell University Press, Gary Young, "Socrates and Obedience," *Phronesis* 19 (1974), 1-29.

Leo Strauss, "On Plato's *Apology of Socrates and Crito*," in Leo Strauss (ed.), *Essays in Honor of Jacob Klein* (Annapolis: St. John's College Press, 1976) and in Leo Strauss, *Studies in Platonic Political Philosophy* (Chicago: University of Chicago Press, 1983, 38-66).

Gerasimos Xenophon Santas, *Socrates: Philosophy in Plato's Early Dialogues* (London: Routledge & Kegan Paul, 1979).

# CHAPTER 6

# BARDAISAN: ON NATURE, FATE, AND FREEDOM

Bardaisan's treatise, now entitled *The Book of the Laws of the Countries*[1] but referred to in antiquity as his dialogue *On Fate*[2], examines the complex interrelationships between nature, fate, and human freedom. This work has received scant philosophical attention[3], however, although it deals in an interesting and novel way with important philosophical issues. What Bardaisan has to say about freedom in relation to nature and fate touches on many of the same philosophical concerns as had previous thinkers (*e.g.* Aristotle in the *Nichomachean Ethics* and the Stoics) and as Augustine has later on in *De libero arbitrio voluntatis*. In many ways Bardaisan's work has unfortunately shared the same neglect as Syriac philosophy, theology, and literature in general.

In order to make Bardaisan's contributions to the study of freedom and the human condition more accessible to philosophical inquiry, this article will explore the following. First of all, because of the relative unfamiliarity of the subject matter in philosophical circles, some background material on Bardaisan himself, his treatise, and Syriac culture in general will be presented. Secondly, a philosophical account of his treatise will be provided. This will focus in part on the structure of the dialogue, showing the systematic development of Bardaisan's position. Critical comments will be made along the way on the steps in Bardaisan's argument. Attention will also be placed on Bardaisan's basic philosophical terminology, chiefly focusing on epistemological, metaphysical, and anthropological expressions. In this way a critical picture of Bardaisan's position on human freedom will be portrayed.

## 1. About Bardaisan

Syriac-speaking culture represents an important, interesting, and complex chapter in the development of Western thought, one that flourished from ca. 200 - ca. 1300 A.D. As a language, Syriac is an Aramaic dialect from the region of Edessa, an area in the upper Euphrates valley, Edessa being the modern Urfu now situated on the Turkish side of the Turkey-Syria border. Syriac came to provide a rather far-flung language of scholarship and thought generally, one that dominated the Christian Middle East and its missions throughout Iran into northern India and China[4]. It was, basically, a Christian culture, first as part of the universal church but later on as Nestorian and Monophysite churches. These churches were condemned as heretical by Western Christianity, and indeed they were at odds with each other. It was not a national culture but existed within many, producing a complex matrix for competing and conflicting cultural influences. As Peter points out,

> Except for an ephemeral and unimportant period as tiny client states to the Roman Empire, the Syriac-speaking community never had a national existence of its own. Its political history is that of the Roman, Byzantine, Sassanian, and Islamic Empires, first as part of the ecumenical Christian community, then as a religious minority.[5]

As a culture, its abiding interest lies not only in the number of original works it produced, Bardaisan's treatise among them, but also as a rich, heterogeneous conduit through which many important works of Greek philosophy and science passed into Islamic society which eventually replaced it as a political and cultural force[6]. Of particular interest here is the transmission of the works of Aristotle.[7] As Arabic became the common language of the educated throughout the

Middle East, the use of Syriac declined, even though the Nestorian and Monophysite churches persisted long into Islamic times. Still, even in the 13th century, two outstanding Syriac thinkers used Syriac for their voluminous writings: the Nestorian scholar 'Abhdiso bar Berikha (Ebedjesu) (d. 1318) and the Monophysite philosopher Bar-Hebraeus (1226-1286) who Rescher notes was "the last important author in this (*i.e.* Syriac) language."[8]

Bardaisan, 154-222 A.D., was the first prominent philosopher of Syriac-speaking culture. He was born in Edessa, of a good family, and associated with the royal court. Edessa was then an independent kingdom, a frontier state between the Roman Empire and the Parthians. Situated on a major trade route, Edessa represented a major multi-cultural center, containing expressions of many philosophical and religious outlooks, both eastern and western. These included Stoicism, eastern Iranian religious movements, Judaism, Christianity, sects of Gnostics, cults of astrology, star-worshippers, *etc.*[9]

Within this rich and variegated society Bardaisan lived, wrote, and taught, attracting a number of students who later formed a prominent and long-lasting school of thought within the region of Edessa. At some point he became a Christian. Later thinkers have had difficulty attaching a label to Bardaisan's own intellectual position, interpreting him variously as a heretic (Ephrem Syrus), as a Gnostic (Hilgenfeld), as an astrologer (Nau), and as a humanist (Schaeder).[10] Perhaps it is truer to say that Bardaisan attempted to develop his own philosophical stance in critical conversation with many religious and philosophical movements of his time. As Drijvers notes:

> ...Bardaisan occupied a unique place in this variegated world, distinguished by high social position and doubtlessly by great erudition, and attempting to bring old and new, East and West, into synthesis.[11]

Towards the end of his life, in 216, Edessa was conquered by Rome and Bardaisan travelled, perhaps to Armenia. He died in 222, although the location is not known. His followers — the Bardaisanites — developed his teachings and became a major intellectual force in Edessa for some time. Ephrem Syrus (306-373) opposed their teachings; Bishop Rabulla of Edessa (d.435) tried to convert them to Christianity; but they were still in existence in the time of Jacob of Edessa (633-708).[12]

Bardaisan seems to have written a great many works. As Eusebius points out,

> ...Bardesanes, a most able man and skilled in Syriac, composed dialogues against the Marcionites and other leaders of various opinions, and he issued them in his own language and script, together with many other of his writings. Those who knew them, and they were many, for he was a powerful arguer, have translated them from Syriac into Greek. Among them is his very powerful dialogue with (pros) Antoninus *Concerning Fate (Peri Heimarmenes)*.[13]

More will be said shortly concerning this "very powerful" dialogue with (or to) Antoninus concerning fate. According to a much later Arabic source, the *Fihrist* of Ibn al-Nadim (ca. 988), Bardaisan wrote works on *Light and Darkness*, *The Spiritual Nature of Truth*, and the *Movable and Immovable*, none of which are now extant. The "Hymn of the Soul" in the apocryphal Acts of Thomas was attributed by some to Bardaisan, but this now seems doubtful.[14] Bardaisan is also said to have composed hymns, still extant in the days of Ephrem Syrus over 100 years later. He is also said to have composed histories of Armenia and India. A brief extract of a treatise on astronomy appears in a letter of George, Bishop of the Arabs (d. 724), taken from an earlier letter of Severus Sebokt (d.666/7).[15] By all accounts, Bardaisan was a prolific author, with many interests.

The treatise now entitled *The Book of the Laws of the Countries* poses some interesting hermeneutical questions. A sixth or seventh-century Syriac manuscript containing this work and others was obtained in 1843 by Archdeacon Tattam from a Syrian convent and deposited in the British Museum (Br. Mus. add. 14,658, *The Book of the Laws of the Countries* occupying columns 129a-141a). It was first mentioned by William Cureton in *Ancient Syriac Versions of the Epistles of St. Ignatius* (1845) and by E. Renan in "Lettre à M. Reinaud" (*Journal Asiatique* 1852). In 1855 Cureton published the Syriac text along with an English translation, a Preface, and notes. In this work Cureton boldly proclaimed:

> The first work printed from this Manuscript is the celebrated Treatise of Bardaisan on Fate, said to have been addressed to the Emperor Marcus Antoninus, commonly known as Marcus Aurelius; although, with the document now complete before us, we find no intimation of its having been so addressed.[16]

Cureton's claim launched a major controversy, the main details of which can be found in Drijvers' indispensable work, *Bardaisan of Edessa*. Prominent among the questions were: Is *The Book of the Laws of the Countries* addressed to Antoninus (as Eusebius says *On Fate* was, although the extant manuscript entitled *The Book of the Laws of the Countries* shows no such address)? In addition, is this Antoninus to be identified with Marcus Aurelius, as Cureton claimed?

Other questions quickly come to the fore as well. Is this work by Bardaisan, or is it by Philip, one of his disciples? Indeed, what could "by Philip" mean: *e.g.* composed as an original work by Philip? compiled by Philip from works by

Bardaisan? transcribed by Philip? *etc.* In each case the use of *The Book of the Laws of the Countries* as a source of information regarding Bardaisan's own position would differ. Moreover, how does the picture obtained of Bardaisan's teachings presented in *The Book of the Laws of the Countries* relate to the teachings of Bardaisan's obtained from other sources, notably the several works of Ephrem Syrus written against Bardaisan's position?[17] In addition, what are the various interrelationships between *The Book of the Laws of the Countries* and extracts of this work found in both Eusebius' *Praeparatio Evangelica* VI, 9, 10 and in the *Recognitions of Clement* IX, 17 and 19-29?

I do not propose to discuss, let alone resolve, these complex issues here but rather to mention these important hermeneutic considerations and to build upon Drijvers' conclusions concerning the salient characteristics of *The Book of the Laws of the Countries*. Drijvers makes the following claims in *Bardaisan of Edessa:*

1. "...the BLC (*i.e. The Book of the Laws of the Countries*) was originally written in Syriac." (p.66)

2. "It was indeed Philippus who wrote down the dialogue, but it remains a dialogue of Bardaisan...." (p.67)

3. The work Eusebius quotes in *Praeparatio Evangelica* and refers to in *Ecclesiastical History* as Bardaisan's "very powerful dialogue with Antoninus Concerning Fate" is the one and the same work, namely Bardaisan's treatise, *The Book of the Laws of the Countries*, dealing with fate. (pp.68-70)

4. Eusebius' addition *"pros Antoninon"* "remains an enigma" (p.69) although it is not Marcus Aurelius'.

5. The work was translated into Greek, as Eusebius says. (p. 74)

6. "The artificial character of the dialogue on Fate, the BLC, must be emphasised. The conversation was never held in this form, we can see that from the whole style....The BLC may therefore be a compilation of various

conversations or treatises of Bardaisan, which originated towards the end of his life or soon afterwards, and which was transmitted under his name." (p.75)

Consequently Cureton's judgment in 1855 that we now have Bardaisan's dialogue *On Fate* seems well supported, and, as such, constitutes the primary source of information now concerning Bardaisan's position on the role of nature and fate in relation to human freedom.

## 2. About The Book of the Laws of the Countries

Superficially *The Book of the Laws of the Countries* appears to be a dialogue, although there are few exchanges between the participants. For the most part, the work consists of a series of seven "considerations," *i.e.* questions or points for Bardaisan to ponder and to respond to. In each case Bardaisan provides a discourse, setting forth his views on the matter at issue. The dialogue is carefully constructed, however, proceeding from

> (a) the importance of the notion of freedom (considerations 1 through 4 inclusive)
>
> (b) the difference between nature and freedom (consideration 5)

and concluding with

> (c) the difference between fate and freedom (considerations 6 and 7).

### Setting

The work begins informally: "A few days ago we went to visit our brother Shemashgram, when Bardaisan came and found us there" (D, p.5).[18] As the discussion ensues, the "we" is identified as including not only Shemashgram and Bardaisan, but also Awida (who, portrayed as one of Bardaisan's new students, asks many of the questions), Philip (who is the narrator of the document we now have), and Bar Jamma (about whom nothing is said). It is not at all clear if all or only some are pupils of Bardaisan. The work begins immediately with Bardaisan asking, "What were you talking about?"

### Consideration I

Those gathered (the "we") reply to Bardaisan's question by reporting that Awida had raised the following question: if God is (a) one, (b) a creator, and (c) expects people to obey his commandments, then why did not God create human beings so that they could not sin but always do what is right?

This question is provocatively formulated, for it does not simply ask what purpose the human capacity to sin serves. Nor does it just inquire why God did not do other than what he did. Given the stress on the unity, creativity, and goodness of God in the question's antecedent, and if it is the case that people do sin and do not always do what is right, then it could follow that somehow this conception of God may not be compatible with the description of actual human conditions. Bardaisan immediately sees the import of Awida's question. Instead of proceeding to answer the why-God-did-not-do-such-and-such portion of the question, he poses an astute counter-question to Awida: does he consider God to be one, or, if one, then such as not to wish humans to behave justly?

Awida has subtly succeeded in putting forth the issue concerning the compatibility of viewing God as one, as creator, and as good, with an understanding of human beings as including a capacity to sin. Bardaisan has replied by raising two possible ways of resolving the dilemma short of defending their compatibility: one is by denying the unity of God (perhaps, then, positing some dualism which could then be used to account for human evil); the other is by affirming the existence of one but an evil God. Either way may represent the real challenge of Awida's question: to use the facts of the human condition (as he and Bardaisan understand them) to force a different conception of God.

## Bardaisan: On Nature, Fate, and Freedom

Awida backs off from answering Bardaisan's counter question, indicating that he wants simply to learn, and, being shy, had initially approached Bardaisan's students rather than the teacher himself personally. Bardaisan commends him, noting that teachers do not question but are questioned and observing that it is excellent for people to know how to formulate questions. Awida reports, however, that Bardaisan's other pupils had not answered his query but only had advised him truly to believe and then he would be able to know everything, anticipating, somewhat, the line of thought expressed by Anselm's *credo ut intelligam*. Awida responds that he cannot believe unless he is convinced.

The issue is whether belief leads to knowledge (as Bardaisan's students say) or whether there must be evidence for belief (as Awida maintains). Bardaisan replies by citing the effects of unbelief: constant analysis and synthesis, lack of knowledge of the truth, an inability to listen, an uncertainty whether one is right in not believing what is not believed, fearfulness, confusion, and rashness. Clearly Bardaisan sides with what his pupils have told Awida the newcomer.

It is unfortunate that Awida is not given the opportunity to respond at this point, for an interesting epistemological debate seems to be in the offing. Belief is distinguished from knowledge; two views concerning the relation of belief to knowledge are advanced; and, indeed, two views of belief are put forward. For Awida, belief requires justification. Rather than providing a basis for knowledge, belief itself must be grounded and justified on the basis of evidence. On this view, belief is itself part of the cognitive process.

Awida's cognitive view of belief differs considerably from Bardaisan's. For Bardaisan, belief is necessary prior to the ferreting out of the pertinent evidence, for belief offers a guideline in the search for knowledge. Cognitive activity is mere groping fumbling without belief. This view of belief might be termed "dispositional," for belief, on Bardaisan's analysis, indicates a believing disposition, one that stabilizes the mind, enabling it to pick out the relevant evidence. It indicates, in other words, an openness to inquiry, but one guided by a framework. On this view, belief is not a cognitive activity but rather a necessary condition for true knowledge.

No more is said explicitly about this important epistemological, and methodological, matter. Superficially it may seem to represent an extraneous digression, a strange interlude in the discussion of Awida's initial question. This appears not to be the case, however, when one compares Bardaisan's insistence here on belief as a disposition to attend to the phenomenon at hand with his own methodological practice in the rest of the dialogue. His own approach is not to start from an assumed truth about the nature of the cosmos but from a willingness to observe the human condition accurately and precisely in order to ascertain what it shows to be true of the world in which we live. His emphasis on belief as a disposition, then, represents a significant shift away from *a priori* speculation about cosmology or anthropology in favor of a much more observational, *a posteriori* account rooted in the very nature of the phenomenon being considered.

Bardaisan returns to Awida's initial question, replying that if God had created human beings so as not to be able to sin, then they would simply be instruments. Here he cites two kinds of instruments. First there are those that like musical instruments or vessels are used by others. Man, however, Bardaisan points out, is like the user of instruments, who has expert knowledge, and it is to this use of things that praise and blame attach. God, he notes, has raised man above many things. Secondly, consider those instruments that are in some ways superior to man: natural objects such as the sun, moon, stars, ocean, mountains, and wind are subject to law and have no choice. Such entities, Bardaisan notes, cannot decide to do or not to do that which they are designed to do. They are "servants and slaves of a single law." (D, p. 13) Man differs from these objects, for to man is

> ...given him to lead his life according to his own free will, and to do all he is able to, if he will, or not to do it, if he will not, justifying himself or becoming guilty. (D, p. 13)

In sum, then, Bardaisan's answer to Awida's question is to point out that human beings (like angels but unlike other creatures) have freedom of choice (*hi'rutha*).

This account is interesting for a number of reasons. First of all, Bardaisan has differentiated human beings from other kinds of entities (God, angels, natural objects, things subservient to man), and he has established priorities: man uses things through knowledge (and for this he is accountable); God uses natural objects through wisdom (and errs not). Secondly, he has answered Awida's question, not by arguing that because man has moral worth or because he is accountable for his use of things that therefore he must be viewed as having freedom of choice. Rather his method of demonstration lies precisely in differentiating kinds of entities and in noting what each has (*e.g.* man has freedom of choice). This again underscores his methodological approach of using observation to generate a theoretical point.

In addition, his view of natural objects is intriguing, especially in the light of various sectors of his own culture and time (astrology, star-worshippers) preoccupied with the influence of such entities on human character, development, and destiny. While clearly focusing on human freedom as freedom to choose, he also emphasizes man's freedom from these natural objects. As instruments of divine wisdom, they are under the control of God; they do not control man. He also adds, however, at the end of this discourse, a note that natural objects, while subject to law, are not completely devoid of freedom and hence will be subject to judgment at The End.

## Consideration 2

Attention is diverted for a moment from human capabilities to a consideration of the implications of Bardaisan's last remark concerning the complex character of natural objects (as subject to law; as not devoid of freedom). Philip asks how entities subject to law can be judged. Bardaisan assures him that these elements (*'estukse';* = Greek *stoicheion*) are judged only insofar as they are free. He explains further that these substances (*'ithe'*) lose part of their inherent power when mixed with one another and in being subject to the power of the creator. They are thus judged only for that "which is their own." (D, p. 15)

The explanation Bardaisan offers is not pursued in any detail, the treatise being concerned with human capabilities rather than cosmology. The conception seems to be that the elements of the universe have a character of their own (including freedom) which is restricted when they form composite substances (such as natural objects) which then possess a new character of their own. Much is left unexplained: *e.g.* why the mingling results in a loss of power; what aspects or parts of these composite substances are not devoid of elemental freedom; the extent to which these composite substances are not devoid of freedom; etc. It is noteworthy, however, that there is no suggestion that the formation of composite substances out of elements is the result of, or indeed the cause of, evil. Moreover, it should be observed that the formation of these natural objects is seen in terms of their being brought under divine control (which would explain their "loss of inherent power" but leave open the question how much inherent power they still retain).

## Consideration 3

Awida does not challenge Bardaisan's answer to his initial question, let alone ask in greater detail how the existence of one good creator God could be compatible with human capacity to sin. Instead he shifts the focus somewhat, but still with the purpose of relating human freedom to divine existence. He

*Bardaisan: On Nature, Fate, and Freedom* 143

notes that the commandments are so onerous that people are incapable of fulfilling them. (The unexpressed conclusion would seem to be that if Bardaisan is right about human freedom, then the one God must be evil, or, at the very least, not serious about the possibility that his commandments be obeyed.)

In reply, Bardaisan at first comments that Awida's observation reflects the viewpoint of one who serves "the enemy of man." (D, p. 15) Next he assures Awida that men are commanded to be only what they are capable of. Two commandments have been placed before people: to avoid evil (*i.e.* what we would not wish to be done to us) and to do good (*i.e.* what we would want to happen to us). Bardaisan notes that carrying out commandments not to steal, not to lie, not to commit adultery, not to hate, *etc.* depends "on man's spirit...on the will of the soul." (D, p. 17) Negatively, he can refrain from evil; conversely, he can do good. None of these, Bardaisan notes, are impossible matters requiring exceptional strength, wealth, or skill. Indeed, he notes, "every human being with a soul can keep them with joy." (D, p. 19)

Awida then asks Bardaisan if he is maintaining that such acts are easily performed. Bardaisan replies that they "are easy for him who so wills." (D, p. 19)

## Consideration 4

Awida suggests that while a person may avoid evil, he may not be able to do what is good. Bardaisan, however, replies that this not the case, contending that "it is much easier to do what is right than to avoid what is wrong." (D, p. 19) In discussing this he distinguishes three kinds of acts.

First of all, there are good acts. Here Bardaisan maintains that good is natural to man, pointing out that doing good occasions joy in the doer, results in a clear conscience, and is something the doer desires to share with others. In addition, there is the avoidance of evil, this being, says Bardaisan, a harder task than the doing of good. He illustrates this by an example: it is easy for someone to praise a friend; harder, however, yet possible to avoid the evil of pouring contempt on an enemy. Finally there are evil acts. These receive an interesting characterization. They are "the work of the enemy," they are done when a person "is not master of himself," that is, when "his true nature is affected." (D, p. 19) Such acts, says Bardaisan, leave a person "troubled and confused, full of anger and fury and tortured in soul and body," (D, p.21) wanting to be seen by nobody.

By this point we have some indication of Bardaisan's conception of human freedom (*hi'rutha*). It is a characteristic of human beings, but not exclusively. God, the angels, and the universal elements also have freedom, but not instruments used by man nor natural objects bound by law except to the degree (unspecified by Bardaisan) that they retain their elemental nature. Freedom involves choice (to do or not to do). The exercise of freedom justifies or condemns the doer, and so it is the source of moral worth.

We have, moreover, a preliminary portrait of Bardaisan's conception of human nature. Man is a composite being, made up of body or flesh (*pagra*) and soul (*naphsha*). There is no suggestion that the body is inferior to the soul, let alone evil. Doing good depends on the will of man's soul. There is no explicit discussion concerning the relationship between body and soul and no suggestion that the soul is immortal. Bardaisan also mentions mind (*r'eyana*) and although its relationship to soul is not clearly indicated, it would appear to represent the thinking, rational aspect of soul.

Finally, at this point, we are left with a puzzle about evil acts. On the one hand, because human beings have free will (to do, not to do) and can do evil, then humans would be responsible for evil acts. On the other hand, Bardaisan characterizes evil as the work of the enemy, evil acts occurring when man is not master of himself, *i.e.* when his true nature is affected. This view seems to attribute evil to an agency outside man. One way to resolve the inconsistency would be to hold that man freely cooperates with the enemy, thereby committing evil acts and thus distorting his true nature. But Bardaisan does not say this.

## Consideration 5

After having argued that people have free will, Bardaisan faces the first of two kinds of deterministic denials of human freedom. Philip reports that Awida had been arguing that people sin by nature (*kyana*) (D, p. 21) on the grounds that if people had not been formed naturally to do wrong, they would not do evil acts. Clearly Awida, the new pupil, is at fundamental odds with Bardaisan.

The kind of deterministic challenge Awida raises is that of "anthropological" or "cosmological" naturalism. Anthropological naturalism might be described as the view that man's behavior is determined by his own constitution (*i.e.* his own nature). Cosmological naturalism would hold that man's behavior is dictated by the whole natural world order (Nature). Bardaisan considers both variants. Both types of naturalism would, of course, rule out human freedom and moral action.

Bardaisan replies that if everyone behaved or thought identically then one could attribute human actions to nature; otherwise not. Again his method of argument is to point out the nature of human behavior and to use it to draw theoretical conclusions, here to deny the adequacy of Awida's naturalism. Bardaisan then proceeds to differentiate nature and freedom, distinguishing in the process between several kinds of nature. The nature (*kyana*) a human exhibits is portrayed as follows: "to be born, grow up, become adult, procreate children and grow old, while eating and drinking, sleeping and waking and finally to die." (D, p. 23) This description is noteworthy, partly because it is cast in functional terms (what humans do) and partly by what it does not include (*e.g.* perceiving, imagining, thinking, *etc.*). These events apply to all human beings and to all living creatures (even, in part, to trees, Bardaisan observes). They are the inherent natural functions of living being. Nature, in one sense, is the basic biological functions of an organism, an aspect of life each member of a species shares with other members.

These functions of life, moreover, are "the work of Nature (*phusis*)," Bardaisan says, "which does, creates and produces everything as it is ordained." (D, p. 23) Here Nature represents a much more comprehensive ordering principle than simply the biological functions of different kinds of organisms. However, not much is said of nature in this second sense here, the word *phusis* being used only twice in the entire dialogue.

Bardaisan makes a further point about the specific nature humans exhibit by citing animal behavior and what it reveals about their nature.

> For the lion is constituted to eat meat, and therefore all lions are carnivores. The sheep eats grass, and therefore all sheep are herbivores. The bee produces honey to subsist on, therefore all bees produce honey. (D, p. 23)

And so on. The general point is that all organisms keep to their distinctive nature: their behavior as members of a species is thus fixed by their nature (*kyana*). The exception is human beings: their lives differ from the fixed pattern exhibited by animals. Bardaisan acknowledges that "in matters pertaining to their body they keep to their natural constitution like the animals do." (D, p. 23) Here he acknowledges the scope of nature (*kyana*) over body, and, to this extent, there is determinism. Bardaisan contends, however, that "as regards matters of their mind, however, they do what they will as free beings, disposing of themselves and as God's image." (D, pp. 23, 25) Humans differ, Bardaisan mentions, concerning food preferences (some prefer meat but no bread; some prefer only certain kinds of meat); sexual behavior (from incest to total abstinence); interpersonal behavior (some take revenge like lions; some stab the innocent like scorpions; some let themselves be victimized like sheep); conduct (good; conformist; evil). So: it cannot be the case that people act entirely because of their nature. In addition to nature, people have free will. To this extent, then, they are exempt from the control of nature.

Bardaisan considers another possibility: suppose someone contends that each person individually has a specific nature which makes him act in a specific way. This represents a third sense of nature, as the expression of one's own individual make-up, a use of *kyana* which seems to exceed sheer biological functions to include all that might properly be termed "one's own." Again this kind of determinism is ruled out because people can change their behavior (*e.g.* the promiscuous or the alcoholic can reform, as can the straight-laced or abstainer) and their minds (*e.g.* those in error can repent and return to the truth).

In sum, then, nature cannot explain all human action; although it governs the body; there is another aspect to man, namely his freedom, and this gives him moral stature. Naturalistic determinism, then, is confined solely to the body and does not extend to the soul and its activities.

## Consideration 6

Philip and Bar Jamma report that some assert that people are ruled by fate (*helqa*). This consideration, of course, would rule out human freedom and might possibly account for the differences in human action Bardaisan has just cited. Along with naturalism, astrological fatalism is another sort of determinism with which Bardaisan must contend. Before advancing his own view, however, Bardaisan surveys various conceptions of the extent of fate over human actions.

First of all he notes that the view Philip and Bar Jamma mention represents the position of the astrologers, a viewpoint that has appeal because of its privileged character (and here he alludes to a previous work) and is indeed one which once interested Bardaisan himself. This position attributes all actions and occurrences to astral influences, specifically to "the Seven Stars." Secondly, others deny the existence of fate, ascribing the differences in behavior and happenings to man's freedom and to chance. Thirdly, others explain everything as the result of human freedom and divine punishment. All these views are partial.

There is fate, says, Bardaisan, for not everything happens according to our will. For example, people desire wealth, power, health, control over circumstances, and yet few experience these and those who enjoy one may not enjoy other good circumstances. It is evident, then, "that riches, honour, health, sickness, children and everything we covet depend on Fate and that we have no power over these matters." (D, pp. 31, 33) So, in explaining human action and happenings that befall man, reference needs to be made to nature, to freedom, and to fate. There is, then, some scope for fate, although it does not rule out the operations of nature or the activities of freedom. According to Bardaisan, the matter can be put succinctly as follows: humans are governed by nature equally, by fate variously, and by freedom as each chooses. (D, p. 33)

The limited scope of fate needs greater examination and so Bardaisan continues the discussion, first to differentiate it from nature, and later on, to distinguish it more clearly from freedom. Fate, according to Bardaisan, is described as follows: "For that which is called Fate is really the fixed course determined by God for the Rulers and Guiding Signs." (D, p. 33) Not much is said here about these Rulers and Guiding Signs — *i.e.* astrological elements — and although they seem to play an intervening role between God and the ordering of the universe it is stressed that they are controlled by God. Fate, however, differs from nature. Nature determines what a person's body is capable of (*e.g.* when child-bearing can begin, when it ceases), what it needs (food, drink), and what it does; fate cannot alter this. Sometimes, Bardaisan says, fate reinforces nature; sometimes it hinders it. Only the latter circumstance is examined, as he classifies what conditions belong to what principle:

## Bardaisan: On Nature, Fate, and Freedom

| Belonging to nature | Belonging to fate |
|---|---|
| human growth and development | illnesses, physical defects |
| sexual intercourse | divorce, impurity, immorality |
| procreation | deformity, miscarriages, |
| sustenance | premature deaths |
| social arrangements | hunger, extravagance, luxury, social disturbances |

So, while it is clear fate cannot alter nature, it can disorder it. As Bardaisan says,

> Be convinced then that whenever nature is deflected from her true course, it is fate that is the cause, because the Rulers and Guiding Signs, from which every change called horoscope is deduced, are in opposition. (D, p. 37)

In sum, then, fate is a legitimate cosmic agency, being that which disturbs the course of nature so as to produce abnormalities within cosmic or anthropological settings. Although his catalogue traces only the malignant effects of fate on nature, Bardaisan would hold that its influence on man is also benign (for, as he has already pointed out, wealth, honor, and health are also attributable to fate).

### Consideration 7

Awida says he is now convinced that people do not sin by nature and that people's behavior varies. He asks Bardaisan to show, though, that people do not act in an evil fashion because of fate and destiny. If he can, says Awida, then it must be admitted that people have freedom to act.

Bardaisan begins his response by pointing out it was because he had shown behavioral diversity that Awida had come to see that people do not sin by nature (Consideration 5). Conversely he will now show that fate cannot account for these aspects of human life to which people conform, *i.e.* social customs.

Bardaisan then commences his famous catalogue of the laws of various societies, from the Chinese, Indians, and Persians in the East, to the Parthians, the Gauls and the Britons in the North (including also the Amazons!). In the course of this recital he makes a number of points to show how compliance with social customs on the part of the individual cannot be explained by recourse to the notion of fate.

For one thing, while social customs vary between societies they are uniform within each society. This the notion of fate cannot explain. If it is contended that people's actions are the result of astral influences, and if these influences are fixed by the position of astral elements at the time of the individual's birth, then one should expect considerable behavioral diversity if the population of a society is born at differing times. This behavioral heterogeneity is not the case, Bardaisan points out, as compliance with social customs and laws indicates.

Secondly, in no case does any astrological element or influence force a person to contravene the social mores of his society. For instance: Mars does not force a Chinese person to kill (where his society prohibits killing); no star forces Brahmins to kill, worship idols, fornicate, eat meat (contrary to their customs in India), and no star forces non-Brahmins in India to follow the Brahmin way of life; no star, moreover, can save male children born in Amazon society.

Thirdly, the absence of certain occupations in some societies cannot be explained by recourse to the notion of fate. For instance, Bardaisan points out, the conjunction of Mercury with Venus in the house of Mercury is alleged to give rise to sculptors, painters and money-changers, and when this conjunction stands within the house of Venus to produce perfumers, dancers, singers and poets. Yet, Bardaisan observes, in a number of societies (*e.g.* Germany, Spain, *etc.*) there are no sculptors, or painters, or perfumers, or money-changers or poets. Bardaisan wonders why "the influence of Mercury and Venus is powerless along the outskirts of the whole world." (D, p. 51)

## Bardaisan: On Nature, Fate, and Freedom

The conclusion is clear:

> In all places, every day and each hour, people are born with different nativities, but the laws of men are stronger than Fate, and they lead their lives according to their own customs. (D, p. 53)

Fate, then, is not a determiner of human action, whether for good or for evil. Rather people exercise the freedom to act they possess. He notes, though, that, as has already been mentioned (Consideration 6), people are subject to fate, and to nature, in virtue of their body.

At this point Philip interjects that this conformity to social customs within each society can be accounted for on one view of fate, namely that view which maintains that the earth is divided into seven "zones" or "climates" (*qlima*; = Greek *klima*), that each of the Seven Stars governs one such region, and that in each climate its power determine social practices.

Bardaisan replies that this view represents an *ad hoc* explanation designed solely to save the theory. Even if the earth were divided into seven climates, he observes, there are not seven kinds of laws to correspond to the Seven Stars (nor 12, nor 36, nor any other convenient astrological number). Moreover, he reminds Philip of other cases where social customs differ or change. In India, for instance, the Brahmins and non-Brahmins follow different customs. Persians (Magians) follow their customs even in different countries. Similarly laws change through conquest (for example, when Rome conquered Arabia it abolished circumcision and other practices). Jews throughout the world, Bardaisan notes, circumcise, observe the Sabbath, *etc.* regardless of the "climate." The same is true of Christians who follow their own customs and do not adopt the repugnant customs of others. As Bardaisan notes in this connection,

> But in whatever place they are and wherever they may find themselves, the local laws cannot force them to give up the law of their Messiah, nor does the Fate of the Guiding Signs force them to do things that are unclean for them. (D, p. 61)

Fate, then, cannot account for human action.

## 4. In Sum

This completes Bardaisan's portrait of the conditions of human existence as depicted in *The Book of the Laws of the Countries*. Man, a soul-body composite, exists in a complex world in which nature, fate, and freedom interact, each having its own legitimate jurisdiction. Man, he points out by way of summary, is governed by nature equally, by fate variously, and by freedom as each chooses. (D, p. 33) He rejects simplistic accounts of the human situation, ones that appeal simply to one sort of principle to explain human action, and in this his philosophical approach is noteworthy. In a time and place dominated by deterministic modes of thought, his careful, analytic, balanced account of human behavior is remarkable for its persistent and forceful defense of human freedom and for its insistence on the instrumentality of the natural world order.

## ENDNOTES

[1]There are three translations of this work: (1) William Cureton, *Spicilegium Syriacum* (London: Rivington, 1855) contains a Preface, Syriac text, notes, and a translation (pp. 1-34); (2) B.P. Pratten in *The Ante-Nicene Fathers*, VIII, American reprint of the Edinburgh Edition (Grand Rapids: Eerdmans, 1951), 723-734); and (3) H.J.W. Drijvers, *The Book of the Laws of the Countries*, translated from the Dutch by Mrs. G.E. van Baaren-Pape (Assen: VanGorcum, 1964) contains both the Syriac text and an English translation. Two other important editions of this text include F. Nau, *Bardesanes Liber Legum Regionum* in *Patrologia Syriaca*, I, 2 (Paris: 1907), 492-658 which contains an extensive introduction, Syriac text, and Latin translation; and F. Nau, *Le Livre des Lois des Pays* (Paris: Geuthner, 1931) which contains the Syriac text and a brief introduction. For the most part I shall use Drijvers' translation, although I shall translate *hi'rutha* as "freedom" rather than (as Drijvers does) as "liberty" so as to avoid the latter's political connotations.

[2]So referred to by Eusebius, Epiphanius, and Theodoretus of Cyrus, among others. See Cureton, *op cit.*, pp. ii, iii.

[3]Two important exceptions are: G. Furlani, "Sur le stoicisme de Bardesane d'Edesse," *Archiv Orientàlnì*, 9 (1937), 347-352; Dom David Amand, *Fatalisme et Liberté dans l'antiquité grecque* (Louvain: Bibliothèque de l'Université, 1945), ch. III "Bardesane le Syrien."

[4]See, for instance, Leonard M. Outerbridge, *The Lost Churches of China* (Philadelphia: Westminster, 1952), ch. II "The First Christians in China."

[5]F.E. Peters, *Aristotle and the Arabs* (New York: New York Univ. Press, 1968), p. 35.

[6]Some details of the transmission of Greek thought into Islamic society through Syriac culture are traced in Max Meyerhof, "Von Alexandrien nach Bagdad," *Sitzungsberichte der Preussischen Akademie der Wissenschaften*, philosophisch-historische Klasse, 23 (1930) and in De Lacy O'Leary, *How Greek Science Passed to the Arabs* (London: Routledge and Kegan Paul, 1949).

[7]See, for instance, G. Hoffmann, *De Hermeneuticis apud Syros* (Leipzig, 1873) which contains the Syriac text and a Latin translation of Probha's Commentary on Aristotle's *De Interpretatione*; Richard J.H. Gottheil, "The Syriac Versions

of the Categories of Aristotle," *Hebraica*, 9 (1892/93), 166-215; Anton Baumstark, *Aristotles bei den Syrern vom V-VIIIten Jahrhundert* (Leipzig: 1900); Khalil Georr, *Les Catégories d'Aristotle dans leurs Versions Syro-Arabes* (Beyrouth: 1948); and Nicholas Rescher, *The Development of Arabic Logic* (Pittsburgh; Univ. of Pittsburgh Press, 1964), 15-22.

[8]Rescher, *op cit.*, p. 206.

[9]For studies in the history of Edessa, see M. Rubens Duval, "Histoire politique, religieuse et littéraire d'Édesse jusqu'à la première croisade," *Journal Asiatique*, 18 (1891), 87-133, 201-278, 381-439 and 19 (1892), 5-102; and J.B. Segal, *Edessa and Harran* (London: School of Oriental and African Studies, 1963).

[10]For an excellent review of previous literature on Bardaisan, see H.J.W. Drijvers, *Bardaisan of Edessa*, trans. Mrs. G.E. van Baaren-Pape (Assen: VanGorcum, 1966), ch. I.

[11]Drijvers, *Bardaisan of Edessa*, p. 217.

[12]For more information on Bardaisan, consult especially Drijvers, *Bardaisan of Edessa; Nau, Bardesanes Liber Legum Regionum*; Anton Baumstark, *Geschichte der Syrischen Literatur* (Bonn: 1922), 12-14; and F.J.A. Hort, "Bardaisan," in W. Smith and H. Wace (eds.), *A Dictionary of Christian Biography* (1877), I, 250-260.

[13]Eusebius, *Ecclesiastical History*, IV, 30. Edition used is translated by Kirsopp Lake (London: Heinemann, 1926).

[14]Drijvers, *Bardaisan of Edessa*, pp. 30, 31, provides the details of F.C. Burkitt's suggestion (1899) and subsequent retraction (1921).

[15]See F. Nau, "Notes d'astronomie syrienne," *Journal Asiatique*, 10ème série, 16 (1910), 209-228.

[16]Cureton, *op cit.*, pp. i, ii.

[17]See C.W. Mitchell, S. Ephraim's *Prose Refutations of Mani, Marcion, and Bardaisan*, vol. I (London: Williams and Norgate, 1912); vol. II completed by A.A. Bevan and F.C. Burkitt (London: 1921).

[18] In this and subsequent quotations, the translation used is that by Drijvers in his *The Book of the Laws of the Countries*.

# PART FOUR:

# A HERMENEUTIC DIRECTION

# CHAPTER 7

# INTERPRETATION, META-INTERPRETATION, AND SOPHOCLES' *OEDIPUS TYRANNUS*

> *Misguided men! What is this foolish war of words You have raised?*

## 1. Interpretation and Meta-Interpretation

It is one thing to interpret a text; it is quite another matter to offer an account of textual interpretation. The first has been called "exegesis," that is, the giving of an interpretation to a text by an interpreter. I shall call this activity, "interpretation." The second has been called "hermeneutics," that is, a view, theory, or account of what constitutes an interpretation or an understanding of a text.[1] This activity represents the development of a view about interpretation, and, as such, is an inquiry at the meta-level. I shall call this second inquiry, "meta-interpretation."

Often the exegetical approach adopted by an interpreter discloses an assumed hermeneutic stance, for there is a close connection between the fruits of interpretation and the meta-interpretive method employed. Yet rarely do interpreters offer interpretation and meta-interpretation in one and the same study.

Bernard M. W. Knox, however, represents an exception to this. In *Oedipus at Thebes*[2] Knox presents an interpretation of Sophocles' *Oedipus Tyrannus*. It is a systematic, well-argued, and provocative interpretation, one that basically views the play as advocating a return to traditional Greek religion and an abandonment of a form of scientific humanism that was becoming popular in the Athens of Sophocles' time.

In presenting this interpretation, Knox also seeks to support and exemplify a specific meta-interpretive position. As he says,

> This book is essentially a study of the Sophoclean play, *Oedipus Tyrannus*, in terms of the age which produced it, an attempt to answer the question, "What did it mean to them, there, then?" But it suggests also an answer to the question, "What does it mean to us, here, now?" And the answer suggested is: the same thing it meant to them, there, then. (pp. 1, 2)

A meta-interpretive position that unabashedly emphasizes that interpretation involves recapturing what it meant to them, there, then seems an ambitious if not impossible project, especially in the light of the contentions of the Heideggerian-style hermeneutics now currently in vogue. Meta-interpretive theorists such as Bultmann,[3] Gadamer,[4] and many others[5] have attempted to work out the implications of historicity for textual understanding and their results would appear to raise serious doubts concerning the feasibility of Knox's project.

At the same time, Knox does not advocate the meta-interpretive alternative to Heideggerian hermeneutics as proposed by Hirsch,[6] namely one that seeks to recover the author's intended meaning as the meaning of the text. In pursuing his meta-interpretive objectives, Knox does not speculate on nor does he try to establish Sophocles' intended meaning in the play. Rather he carefully examines the text itself, situating it in the context of movements in the age in which the play was performed in order to arrive at an understanding of what it means.

In explicitly bringing to the fore the question of what the text meant to them, there, then, Knox is putting forward a view which essentially represents a third meta-interpretive option. This option, which might be dubbed a "hermeneutics of fidelity," is one that focuses on the text of the play itself and its meaning in the context of its original production. Coming as it does from classical scholarship, this view is interestingly paralleled in New Testament scholarship in the writings of Oscar Cullmann, for instance, contends:

> I emphasize here only that I know no other "method" than the proven philological-historical one. I know of no other "attitude" toward the text than obedient willingness to listen to it even when what I hear is sometimes completely foreign, contradictory to my own favorite ideas, whatever they may be....[7]

and in this Cullmann is espousing a hermeneutics of fidelity.

Is it possible to steer a hermeneutic course between the Charybdis of historicity (and its alleged implications for understanding) on the one hand and the Scylla of the author's intended meaning as constitutive of the text's correct meaning on the other? In other words, is a third meta-interpretive option possible?

It would be an enormous undertaking, of course, to attempt to construct a hermeneutics of fidelity to the text. Much remains unclear about the nature of textual interpretation at both the interpretive and meta-interpretive levels. I shall not attempt such a construction. There are, however, several preliminary and prior matters that need to be probed much more closely before such a construction could be attempted. These matters I will examine.

In this article I am concerned with two main questions, one at the level of interpretation and one at the meta-interpretive level. I use the former to open up the latter, it being my conviction that interpretation has (or ought to have) an important bearing on meta-interpretation. At the level of interpretation I ask, of a particular text,

(1) what does it mean?

The text I have selected for interpretive scrutiny is Sophocles' *Oedipus Tyrannus*.[8] I examine various attempts to answer this question with respect to this text, and, in so doing, I sketch the outlines of a major interpretive controversy. Section 2 of this paper examines Knox's interpretation of the play; section 3 then presents several quite different understandings of the play, at least one of them being incompatible with Knox's interpretation.

I start with a particular interpretive controversy chiefly for two main reasons. First of all, it is out of a heterogeneity of meanings that question (1) takes on a problematic status. Secondly, I find that there are certain facets of the controversial nature of textual interpretation that suggest a direction for meta-interpretive reflection, facets which have been largely overlooked hitherto.

In attempting to answer question (1), I find a great variety of responses, some of them incompatible with one another. I then move (in section 4 of this paper) to ask a different sort of question, namely,

>   (2) what are we to make of the situation whereby question (1) receives as an answer that the text has been given a variety of different interpretations?

In the light of a meta-interpretive direction that grows out of noting certain facets of interpretive controversy, I examine (in section 5 of this paper) various aspects of question (2). I point out the pentadic structure of textual interpretation, the importance for meta-interpretation of a study of interpretive arguments, and I suggest a way in which a logic of textual interpretation could be developed. In this way some problematic features of questions (1) and (2) are opened up and clarified.

In sum this paper sets out to do three things: to present an interpretive controversy, to examine the theoretical import of the sort of interpretive

*Interpretation, Meta-Interpretation and Sophocles'...* 163

controversy that results in interpretive diversity (and incompatibility), and to suggest a new meta-interpretive direction, one that arises from the controversial nature of textual interpretation itself and which emphasizes the central role of interpretive arguments.

Before venturing into meta-interpretation, let us begin by focusing on the interpretation of one particular text, namely Sophocles' *Oedipus Tyrannus*, and let us ask in all naiveté, what does it mean?

## 2. Knox's Interpretation of Oedipus Tyrannus

Knox presents the following argument in support of his interpretation of *Oedipus Tyrannus*. For ease of reference subsequently, the argument will be referred to as "argument A" and the main points will be numbered and referred to as "A-claims":

A1. In the play, Oedipus' will is free. (pp. 5,12)

Knox rejects the popular interpretive view that the play is a tragedy of fate. Indeed, he claims, "in the actions of Oedipus in the play 'fate' plays no part at all" (p. 60). Knox is aware, of course, that this view is highly controversial and he is careful to consider, and subsequently reject, three possible counterclaims to A1.

For one thing, early on in the play, Tiresias announces in his presence that Oedipus murdered Laius. he also predicts both Oedipus' discovery and blindness. It might be argued, on this basis, that the play is therefore a fulfillment of this prophecy and a demonstration of the power and truth of fate.

Knox rejects this construal. Tiresias' utterance, he points out, is not an external force operating on Oedipus. Tiresias speaks, but only under duress, against his firm resolve not to speak, and in response to Oedipus' provocation. It is, moreover, without effect: Tiresias' prophetic utterance has no effect, Knox contends, on Oedipus' subsequent action. His prophecy thus does not make anything happen.

Secondly, Knox points out that Tiresias explicitly says, "No — it is not I who will cause your fall. That is Apollo's office — and he will discharge it" (pp. 376, 377). Here Oedipus' downfall is specifically attributed to the causal agency of Apollo. On this basis it might be argued that Oedipus' catastrophe is simply the result of divine activity.

Again Knox rejects this construal. He points out that modern translations of this passage depend on a 1786 emendation of the text by Brunck, noting that the original text states in effect, "if I am to fall, that is Apollo's business and he can take care of it" (p. 8). Knox also adds that an emendation ought not to be accepted unless the original does not make sense which, in this case, it does.

Thirdly, Knox observes that

> it might also be urged that the process of Oedipus' self-discovery starts with his request to the Delphic oracle for advice about the plague, that the plague is therefore the causal factor, and the Plague is sent by Apollo, who in this play represents the external factor, "fate." (pp. 8, 9)

There is no suggestion, however, as Knox points out, that Apollo is responsible for the plague. Apollo's priest prays at the outset for Apollo to rescue the city from the plague but he does not thereby connect Apollo with having caused the plague in the beginning. The Chorus, moreover, attributes the plague to Ares and regards Apollo, along with Athena, Artemis, and Dionysus as allies in the struggle. The plague, therefore, is not the manifestation of fate. That there is an initial plague is, however, important, for it represents a problem that prompts Oedipus into action.

Not only are Oedipus' actions not presented by Sophocles as fated, they are, on the contrary, presented as stemming from a decisive man of action, a person who is clearly capable of thinking for himself and of making decisions. He decides, for instance, to hear Creon's report from the oracle in public; he decides to search for the murderer of Laius; he decides, even before the chorus suggests it, to consult Tiresias; he decides, moreover, to proceed with the investigation even though counselled four times against doing so. Oedipus is free, not fated.

This has important consequences for the development of the plot. As Knox points out, "Oedipus' action is not only the action of a free agent, it is also the cause of the events of the play" (p. 12). The events that take place in the play occur because of Oedipus' actions. It is his relentless pursuit of the truth, and the decisions he makes along the way, that set in motion and sustain the plot. So, in addition to A1, Knox also contends:

> A2. The decisions and actions of Oedipus are the causal factors in the plot of the tragedy. (p. 14)

Not only that, but Knox also maintains:

> A3. These decisions and actions are the expression of the character of Oedipus. (p. 14)

What, then, is the character of Oedipus? Knox discusses this at length (pp. 14-29), essentially portraying him as a man of decision and action. Oedipus reflects, deliberates, and interrogates. Three times he skillfully examines a witness (Creon, the messenger from Corinth, the shepherd). He demands a rational basis for his beliefs, countenancing, Knox points out, "no mysteries, no half-truths, no half-measures" (p. 18). He is by no means portrayed as a passive pawn in the operations of a relentless fate.

Knox asks, "From what aspects or aspect of the hero's character do the decisive actions spring?" (p. 29). He locates it precisely on "his intelligence, which will accept nothing incomplete, nothing untested, only the full truth" (p.

30). As Knox points out, Oedipus refuses to accept Tiresias' insistence that he drop the whole matter; he refuses to accept Jocasta's suggestion to let matters lie following the arrival of the Corinthian messenger. In each case Oedipus presses on with the inquiry. Here, says Knox, "he is most himself" (p. 30). It is on this basis that Knox makes the following claim:

> A4. The catastrophe of Oedipus is a product not of any one quality of Oedipus but of the total man.
> (p 31)

The actions that occur in the play come about not because of any one flaw in the make-up of Oedipus (and it is here, on the basis of A4, that Knox rejects Aristotle's interpretation of the play) but rather because Oedipus as a whole is the sort of person he is. There is catastrophe in the play, to be sure, but it is one that shocks the reader or hearer because of its enormity, not because it is linked to any *hamartia* in the character of Oedipus.

The meaning of the play, therefore, does not lie in the role of fate (A1 precludes this) nor does it lie in any one fatal flaw inherent in Oedipus' character (precluded by A4). Where, then, is the meaning of the play to be found?

It is clear what Oedipus learns in the course of the play. As Knox points out,

> What he discovers in the play is not only that he is his father's murderer and his mother's husband, but that he has long ago fulfilled to the letter the prediction which he thought he had so far dodged, and which, at the height of his hope, he thought he had escaped forever. (p. 33)

This directs our attention to an element outside Oedipus' decisions and actions which also plays a significant role in the play: the role of prophecy. The actions whose true nature Oedipus comes eventually to understand have been predicted. They had been predicted to Laius and then to Oedipus as a youth.

*Interpretation, Meta-Interpretation and Sophocles'...* 167

That the major events in Oedipus' life had been predicted must be carefully understood. This is not to say, as Knox is at pains to point out, that Oedipus' actions are in any sense caused by divine agency:

> ...in the *Oedipus Tyrannus* Sophocles has chosen to present the terrible actions of Oedipus not as determined but only as predicted, and he has made no reference to the relation between the predicted destiny and the divine will. (p. 38)

Nor is it to say that prophecy and prophecy alone is the causal agency at work in the play. Rather the plot is much more complicated and subtle, for it is the combination of prophecy along with, and in interaction with, Oedipus' character that eventually produces the outcome.

According to Knox, the meaning of the play is therefore to be located in the complex interaction between prophecy and Oedipus' character. Specifically, it is to be found in terms of how Oedipus himself responds to and copes with the prophetic declaration concerning his life. As Knox puts it:

> The meaning...is emphasized by Sophocles' presentation of the given situation, the action of the hero, and the nature of the catastrophe. The factor common to all three is a prophecy, a prophecy given, apparently defied, and finally vindicated. (p. 42)

It is this that provides the clue for understanding the play. Knox follows this clue:

A5. In the play, Oedipus
 (a) receives a prophecy;

This is vital for understanding the play. For, as Knox stresses, what Oedipus has done makes sense only in the context of the prophecy that spans Oedipus' life as a whole. It is what gives his parricide and incest meaning.

> A5. (continued) In the play, Oedipus
> (b) apparently defies a prophecy;

The play, as Knox views it, stresses Oedipus' defiance of prophecy. At the outset Oedipus appears to be a person who has "attempted to prove the Oracle a liar" (p. 43), apparently successfully. In this Oedipus is attempting to undermine not just prophecy but the whole religious tradition and outlook. It is the truth of divinity that Oedipus challenges by his actions. The Chorus points out this aspect of the awesome significance of Oedipus' efforts: if the oracles fail in veracity, then religious observances and obedience go by the board (ll. 897-910).[9]

Oedipus directly attacks prophecy, and, thereby, traditional religion. For one thing, he mocks Tiresias, the representative of the god Apollo. Where were you when the Sphinx harassed the city, Oedipus taunts, and replies that it was by his wit that the city was saved. Jocasta, moreover, openly rejects prophecy as "worthless" and for this she has proof. With this Oedipus concurs (although, to be sure, he sends for the shepherd, just to confirm the details of her proof). Jocasta extends her point of view, rejecting divine order and sovereignty: "chance rules supreme" (ll. 977-8). With this view Oedipus does not immediately concur but presses on with the inquiry. It is only at the very point that Jocasta discovers her error and ignorance that Oedipus comes around to the very position she herself has just abandoned, proclaiming himself "the child of Fortune" (l. 1080), thereby, too, denying divine order and rule.

> A5. (continued) In the play, Oedipus
> (c) learns eventually that prophecy cannot be so defied.

He learns that the very actions predicted of him have long since come true. Moreover,

> A6. Oedipus is like the person of Sophocles' own day who scoffs at religion, who favors arrogant humanism of the sort expressed for example in Protagoras' dictum that man is the measure of all things, and who needs to learn that such a view is ignorant and false. (pp. 44-47)

The play, says Knox, "takes a clear stand on one of the intellectual battlegrounds of the fifth century — the question of the truth or falsehood of prophecy" (pp. 43, 44). With Herodotus defending prophecy, and Thucydides, Euripides and Protagoras attacking it in one way or another, the issue was very much alive in Sophocles' own day. As Knox points out, the issue was a broad and vital one: "The question at issue in the debate was not just the truth or falsehood or prophecy, but the validity of the whole traditional religious view" (p. 46). The whole intellectual development in the play, with Oedipus' and Jocasta's mockery of prophecy to the affirmation of chance, with the tremendous emphasis on inquiry and one's own reason, stands as a symbolic representation of fifth-century Greek rationalism. It is a view, however, which according to Knox, Sophocles rejects.

As Knox construes it, the play is a demonstration of the futility of such humanistic rationalism. On the basis of A1 to A6, Knox concludes:

> The play is a terrifying affirmation of the truth of prophecy (and, consequently, of the whole traditional religious outlook). (p. 43)

Oedipus is presented by Sophocles as an "example" (l. 1193) — an example to all of divine existence, sovereignty, and knowledge on the one hand, and of human ignorance and limitation on the other. Put more expansively, Knox claims:

> The play...is a reassertion of the religious view of a divinely ordered universe, a view which depends on the concept of divine omniscience, represented in the play by Apollo's prophecy. It is a statement which rejects the new concept of the fifth-century philosophers and sophists, the new visions of a universe ordered by the laws of physics, the human intelligence, the law of the jungle, or the lawlessness of blind chance. (p. 47)

## 3. Alternate Interpretations of *Oedipus Tyrannus*

The play may be viewed in quite a different light than the interpretation given it by Knox. In this section I shall develop and defend another line of interpretation (it is my own), one that stresses the role of inquiry in the play and which views Oedipus as a model inquirer. For ease of reference I shall refer to this line of interpretation as "argument B" and the main points as "B-claims."

Argument B goes as follows;

> B1. In the play,
> (a) Oedipus persistently and relentlessly searches for the whole truth concerning the devastation that ravishes the city;

The play opens with a host of problems that require solution. For one thing, there is a commotion in front of an altar outside his palace, and Oedipus must deal with this. Then, more importantly, there is death and devastation throughout the city. Oedipus inquires, ponders, and acts.

The play thus begins by drawing our attention to two salient features of Oedipus' character: he is a rigorous inquirer and a decisive decision-maker. He sizes up and deals with situations in a resolute manner. He finds out what is wrong and then decides and acts. He finds out, for example, at first hand why the people are raising a commotion. He had, moreover, already taken steps to find a solution to Thebes' trauma — even before the populace undertook processions to various religious shrines. The problem was already well under consideration.

Oedipus is presented not only as the inquirer but also as the suffering inquirer. Sophocles stresses this. Oedipus is heartbroken over the devastation of Thebes. Out of this suffering he seeks to find out what he can say or do — that is, to learn what is within his power to alter. This, indeed, is the very question he puts to the Oracle. The Oracle, however, does not answer this question but rather the more general question, namely, what must be done to alleviate the devastation.[10] In so doing it links the devastation to an unavenged murder.

The Prologue and the *parados* or opening choric recitative which immediately follows it presents four different approaches to inquiry. The Chorus, for example, views the situation in theological terms: the situation is the result of Ares' activity, and the solution is to be found in calling for divine assistance (Athena, Artemis, Apollo, Dionysus) to save the city. The Chorus thus rejects inquiry.

The priest of Zeus, however, adopts a somewhat different stance. While calling upon Apollo to save the city, he also appeals to Oedipus to help, as being someone who had previously found a way to aid the city. He does not dismiss human help (as does the Chorus) but his approach to problem-solving is authoritarian in nature; seek the one who heroically, mysteriously, and single-handedly can deliver the city from affliction. Yet, like the Chorus, the priest of Zeus simply asks, who can save us? the difference being simply that in the latter instance, the "who" includes human as well as divine agency.

Creon, however, typifies a third approach to inquiry. He admits that it was a preoccupation with present concerns (the Sphinx) that had prevented a full-scale investigation into the cause of Laius' death. This approach represents aborted inquiry: it is not a rejection of inquiry *per se*, as in the previous two cases, but it does portray inquiry as shunted aside by lesser but more pressing concerns.

Oedipus alone represents resolute inquiry. He finds out what the situation is (it is the presence of an unknown assassin within the city, not the presence of Ares). He mulls over alternate solutions — indeed, he is the only one who is presented as thinking about the situation: "I...set my thoughts on countless paths, searching for an answer" (l. 67). He asks what is within his power to say or do that would alleviate the situation. He steadfastly determines to probe relentlessly for the unknown assassin. Oedipus is the inquirer: he does not claim to know. He knows he does not know and resolves, simply, to find a solution to the problem, as best he can.

> B1. (continued)In the play
> (b) Oedipus patiently puts together the various pieces of the puzzle by reasoning out the connections and demanding proof.

This characteristic, established at the outset in Oedipus' search for a way out of the Theban devastation, is reinforced in his rejection of Tiresias' edict. Tiresias' oracular pronouncement indicts Oedipus. But it is simply that: a claim without supporting evidence. Oedipus rejects this declaration. For one thing, he dismisses this unexpected — and unsubstantiated — answer as unprophetic and he attacks Tiresias' credentials. In addition, he questions the answer's rationality. After all, Oedipus himself, by his wit, *had* been able to solve the Sphinx's riddle when Tiresias could not. How, then, could Tiresias legitimately claim to know the truth? But, most importantly, the answer does not make sense unless — and here Oedipus' reasoning runs ahead of us — Tiresias and Creon are in conspiracy against him. What else could account, after all, for Tiresias' charge? In terms of what Tiresias has said, Oedipus' surmise is logical. Even the Chorus rejects Tiresias' claim, pointing out that while Zeus and Apollo may know, mortals do not, and citing Oedipus' success with the Sphinx.

Tiresias adamantly refuses to divulge the basis for his pronouncement, the very thing Oedipus demands. Without grounding, Tiresias' pronouncement is ineffectual and worthless. Indeed, while what Tiresias says is true, the truth is realized only as the result of a very different process. Truth is not perceived through divine utterance but by diligent, painstaking, all-too-human inquiry that takes many turns until the truth is brought to light by the interrogation of first-hand witnesses.

Rejection of the truth of Tiresias' claim does not mean, however, that Oedipus fails to take it seriously. He does, as the next scene in the play shows. In getting to the bottom of Tiresias' charge, Oedipus starts his inquiry off on the wrong track. He harangues Creon who admits he advised Oedipus to send for Tiresias, that he investigated the murder of Laius a long time ago, and that Tiresias had never then made any allegations against Oedipus. So, Oedipus concludes, if Tiresias had not acted under Creon's instructions, he would not have named Oedipus as Laius' assassin.

What seems here like a squabble — a "foolish war of words," as Jocasta puts it — is really a disclosure of the alacrity and astuteness of Oedipus' logical mind. He reasons (1) either Creon must be guilty of treachery or else he himself must be guilty (as Tiresias declared). He knows (2) he is not himself guilty. No evidence has been brought forward to counter this supposition. Thus it would follow, from (1) and (2), that Creon is at fault. The argument is valid. Indeed, as Oedipus points out the Chorus, if they fully understood what they were asking when they beseeched him to respect Creon's solemn oath and his past integrity, they are indirectly — and logically — accusing him of the guilt (ll. 655-9), for, according to Oedipus' first premise, the alternative to Creon's treachery is his own guilt. The Chorus recoils in confusion, but does not know how to exonerate both Creon and Oedipus.

The investigation then takes a different direction. Rather than advancing a conspiracy-hypothesis, Jocasta attempts to prove the powerlessness of divination and thus the baselessness of Tiresias' declaration. This unsettles Oedipus. He suspects the truth ("Am I cursed and cannot see it?" ll. 744-5) but he is reluctant to admit it ("It cannot be — that the prophet sees" l. 747). He presses on with the investigation. He reasons that if the shepherd stated that robbers killed Laius, then he would be freed. As Jocasta points out, however, even if the shepherd changes his story and singles out an individual, Oedipus would still be exonerated, for Apollo had said Laius would be killed by his own son. With Oedipus pressing on with the investigation by sending for the shepherd, the Chorus piously praises the pure, immortal laws of Olympus and chides "seeking things unseasonable, unreasonable" (l. 875), thereby rejecting inquiry and advocating traditional religious obedience.

    B1.  (continued)In the play
        (c) Oedipus eventually finds out the answer.

Gradually the pieces fall into place as Oedipus quizzes the Corinthian messenger and the shepherd, against all advice and in spite of their hesitation. Finally Oedipus knows — "I see it now" (l. 1182). He sees it only when the alternatives have been explored and when every piece has been testified to by eye-witnesses, that is, only when corroborated and grounded in personal veracity. The Chorus begins a lament — men are nothing, wretched Oedipus, Time found him out, etc. — and here the Chorus is way off-target. It was not Time who found Oedipus out; it was, on the contrary, Oedipus who found out. The truth was the result of *his* active searching, not his passively having been sought out by Time. The Chorus completely misdescribes the situation here.

> B1. (continued) In the play
>
> (d) Oedipus accepts the answer, no matter how painful and unexpected the truth is.

Oedipus' first inclination is to blame fate (l. 1311) or Apollo (l. 1329), indeed, even the shepherd (ll. 1349, 50), but he soon rallies, emphasizing his role in blinding himself, in condemning himself, in doing what he had to do. He takes command of the situation, telling Creon to cast him out, arranging with Creon for Jocasta's funeral, and asking him to care for his daughters. He is very much the old Oedipus — but with a difference: he now knows the truth and he has accepted it and its consequences.

The Chorus concludes with a farewell — "there goes Oedipus" — portraying him as a man who, once mighty and gifted, is now "drowning in waves of dread and despair" (l. 1527). Again the Chorus has misrepresented the situation: Oedipus, far from drowning, is thoroughly in charge of the situation. But notice: the Chorus is still unable to see what Oedipus has accomplished. They fail to see that it is the same Oedipus who was able to answer the Sphinx's riddle. The Chorus is blind to the Oedipus who searched, found out, and who has come to terms with the truth that he, by his wit, has uncovered.

> B2. In this process, Oedipus has moved from the level of Appearance to the level of Reality; he has learned that man's life is in reality not free but fated; and he learns to live with this truth, in spite of its unpleasantness and unexpectedness.

Throughout the play there is an interesting contrast between Oedipus and the chorus. The Chorus never advances in understanding. It never moves beyond a passive, unquestioning reliance on divine law and order. It calls upon a litany of gods/goddesses for help; it stresses obedience to the laws of heaven and disaster to those who defy these laws. It rejects inquiry; and it sees in Oedipus a man whom Time has found out. It articulates the whole posture of theological dependence.

This point of view has three consequences. For one thing, the Chorus is helpless: it cannot do anything to improve the situation in Thebes. Secondly, it cannot see the activity of Oedipus and the process he undergoes, as he passes from ignorance to knowledge through inquiry, thereby solving the problem that plagued the city. Finally, it misunderstands the situation, for it cannot see, let alone value, the process whereby knowledge is accrued and truth disclosed. The Chorus learns, understands and sees nothing, and this is a consequence of its intellectual stance.

Oedipus, in contrast, grows in understanding. What seems at the outset to be a search for an unknown assassin becomes, in reality, a self-discovery of the truth about oneself. The problem, which at the outset appears to be Thebes' problem, is seen at the end to be Oedipus' problem. Oedipus has moved from the level of Appearance to the level of Reality. And he has done so through inquiry.

What Oedipus learns is that Reality is vastly different from Appearance — indeed, his whole world has been turned upside-down, socially, personally, and intellectually. The truth is quite other than what appears initially to be the case. It is much more self-involving, less predictable, more surprising, than he had hitherto thought. He also learns that, in spite of free, rational decisions, aided by acute logic, he has already fulfilled in his life what was predicted of his actions. In Appearance, he is free; in Reality, he is fated. This is not to say that there is a contradiction here between freedom and fate, any more than there is one between not-knowing and knowing. Rather Oedipus' knowledge at the end is torn from the deceptions and falsehoods of Appearance and elevated to the apprehension of the truths of Reality. The truth is painful, burdensome, and alienating, and Oedipus must adapt. We see him at the end, beginning this adaptation, leaving others behind.

> B3. Oedipus, then, is like the humanist seeker after truth of Sophocles' own time, the one who relentlessly pushes inquiry beyond customarily accepted opinions to the truth beyond, no matter what the personal cost, and who accepts this truth, no matter how unpalatable or how unpredictable.

Ever since the days of Heraclitus and Parmenides, it had been known (1) that there is a gap between Appearance and Reality, and (2) that Reality is quite unlike Appearance. The natural philosophers before Heraclitus and Parmenides, and especially the Pythagoreans, had encountered this, for both the principle of unity and the principle of differentiation were quite unlike anything met by the senses. Parmenides in particular drove the wedge deeply between the two: the Way of Opinion, the way of change and of opposites, which cannot be thought, and is not, on the one hand; and the Way of Truth, the way of the changelessly eternal, on the other. What is, is vastly different from what is commonly (and erroneously) supposed to be: Reality is

> "unbegotten...imperishable...whole...immovable...comp
> lete    ...since it is now, all at once, one and continuous."[11]

Sophocles, too, exploits the difference between Appearance and Reality and he shows us a person in movement, one who successfully makes the transition into Reality. In so doing, Sophocles contributes at least three very significant points to the ongoing discussion.

For one thing, he portrays the power of inquiry, for it is the means by which Appearance is transcended. The Chorus, for example, never attains this state but remains locked in to the illusions and distortions of appearance. And while Tiresias may have apprehended the Truth directly and Jocasta may have intuited it indirectly, in neither case is true opinion grounded in knowledge.[12]

Finally, the passage from Appearance into Reality exacts a tremendous price: deep personal pain and anguish, the sort of horrible suffering Oedipus undergoes so acutely. It is truth that his inquiry is launched in suffering, but it ends in a suffering of a much greater intensity. *Oedipus Tyrannus* is pre-eminently a play that demonstrates the profound personal cost of inquiry.

In many ways, Sophocles' play anticipates the message of the Cave Allegory in Plato's *Republic*.[13] Both stress the move from Appearance to Reality, the crucial role of inquiry, the otherness and unfamiliarity of Reality, the alienation and solitariness the rational pursuit of Reality entails, and the high personal pain of such a pursuit. Both make the same epistemological point and both do so dramatically.

Oedipus, then, is like the seeker after truth in Sophocles' own time. He is the one who trusts in reason, logic, and inquiry to open up and uncover the truth that lies hidden, one who takes clues from but who is not bound by the dictates of religious insight. Such an inquirer is not only persistent, relentless, and courageous; he is also a sufferer, alienated, and lonely, for that is the personal cost of seeking Truth.

On this line of interpretation, claims B1 - B3, the following conclusion is reached about the meaning of the play:

> *Oedipus Tyrannus* is a story about the dreadful agony of human inquiry and the horrible price paid for growth in knowledge and true understanding.

As is readily evident, argument B differs considerably from argument A.

There are, of course, other quite different interpretations of *Oedipus Tyrannus*. Omitting the discussion such a view would obviously require, one timely but somewhat facetious interpretation goes as follows (let us refer to this as "argument C"):

> C1. Both Oedipus and Jocasta seek to outwit a prophecy.
>
> C2. In the course of the play, both Oedipus and Jocasta
> (a) discover that they have not succeeded in outwitting the prophecy, and
> (b) respond in their own way to this discovery.
>
> C3. Oedipus discovers the truth by dint of slow patient reasoning; Jocasta, by a quick, perceptive, intuitive realization.

---

> The play shows the superiority of intuitive reasoning over methodical deduction.

This argument, focusing more than traditional views of the play do on Jocasta and the process she undergoes, produces quite a different interpretive thrust from arguments A and B.

In addition, Philip Vellacott has recently offered a new interpretation of *Oedipus Tyrannus*, one that develops an interesting and challenging interpretive alternative to Knox's position and what Vellacott calls the traditional view.[14] According to Vellacott, the traditional view holds that Oedipus is ignorant of his true identity, at least up to l. 716 ("at a junction of three highways"). He disputes this view. Without doing justice to the richness of his discussion on behalf of each main point, his argument can be briefly sketched as follows (let us refer to this as "argument D"):

> D1. There are six questions which (in Vellacott's judgment) have never been properly answered. (see pp. 114ff)
>
> D2. These questions can be accommodated if we suppose
> (a) that on the surface the play presents Oedipus as ignorant of his true identity, and yet
> (b) that "beneath the surface" the play shows "with complete clarity" that "Oedipus knew as soon as he had entered Thebes who it was he had killed, and was aware of his parricide and incest from the first night of his marriage."(p. 129)
>
> D3. There is evidence for D2(b).

---

> Sophocles intended the *careful reader* (and perhaps some unusually acute spectators) to see Oedipus as having been aware of his true relationship to Laius and Jocasta ever since the time of his marriage." (p. 104)

The support for premise D3, a crucial one, is provided by a detailed study of each portion of the play (see pp. 125-46) and comes from clues provided in Oedipus' discussions with Tiresias, Creon and Jocasta (*e.g.*, in Oedipus' "flying off the handle" at Tiresias and Creon); in what Oedipus, Creon and the Chorus do not say (e.g., in not suggesting that the "one man who ran away" from the murder of Laius — l.118 — be summoned immediately and interrogated); and in what Oedipus would undoubtedly have realized upon entering Thebes and marrying Jocasta. The play thus becomes, on this line of interpretation, a study of the terror of admitting to oneself and to others the truth about oneself, a truth one in a sense knows, and yet, because of a carefully cultivated facade, one knows not.

## 4. Interpretations: Diversity, Conflict, and Incompatibility

In the preceding two sections, a particular interpretive controversy has been examined. Four different interpretive positions on Sophocles' *Oedipus Tyrannus* have been sketched, two of them (A and B) in some critical detail. We started out by asking in all naiveté, what does Sophocles' *Oedipus Tyrannus* mean? In reply, we were greeted with a great variety of answers. Arguments A, B, C, and D present four quite different views concerning what the play means, as their respective conclusions clearly indicate. I take this situation of interpretive diversity to be typical of interpretive controversies generally. Put schematically, the typical answer to the question (call it "question I"):

(I) What does text t mean?

is of the form:

(i) Text t means interpretation $i_1$, interpretation $i_2$, ...,interpretation $i_n$.

(or, to put it more tersely, t means $i_1, i_2,...,i_n$).

An answer to this sort of question (I) may be found to be overwhelming. Indeed, an answer of form (i) is very difficult to construe. For instance, in asking question (I), we may have initially expected in reply an answer of quite another sort, one having the following form:

(ii)   t means $i_x$.

or, at worst, some slight divergence in meanings. Yet the conclusions to interpretive arguments A, B, C, and D differ markedly as to the play's meaning. They forbid any answer to (I) along the lines indicated by form (ii). We are confronted, then, with having to make sense of an answer of form (i) to question (I).

The situation whereby an answer of form (i) is regarded as the answer to question (I) may be variously construed. Some may argue that an answer of form (i) is all one can expect to question (I), plays, persons, and interpretations being what they are. On this approach one would simply have to reform one's expectations to correspond to the alleged exigencies of the interpretive situation.

Even so, on this approach, one would still be left with the question how (i) is an informative answer to question (I), let alone whether it is an answer to (I) at all. Others would contend, moreover, that there is something wrong with an answer of form (i), namely that it is not an answer to the question asked. It is simply unresponsive, this approach contends, to answer the question, "what does text t mean?" with a catalog or series of meanings. An "answer" of form (i) represents, on this view, an inability or a refusal to answer the question posed. Shortly (in section 5 of this paper) I shall argue that this latter view, somewhat modified, is correct, for an interesting reason not yet apparent.

There is another puzzling aspect of an answer of form (i) which may be expressed formally as follows: how are the commas in the answer to be interpreted, as "and" or as "or"? If the former, then an answer of form (i) would that a text t means interpretation $i_1$ and interpretation $i_2$ and so on. Are we therefore to accept the view that the text means each and every interpretation it is given? This would appear to be a position congruent with the view that an answer of form (i) is all one can expect to question (I).

If, on the other hand, the commas in (i) are construed as "or" (in its exclusive sense), then the answer is viewed as setting forth a variety of alternative meanings for the text. This immediately raises the specter of selection, for to say of a text t that it means interpretation $i_x$ or (exclusive sense) interpretation $i_y$ or (exclusive sense) interpretation $i_z$ is either to say that some interpretation or interpretations are to be accepted and others not, or to say that none of these interpretations are to be accepted, but not to say that all interpretations are to be accepted. When viewed along these lines, interpretive diversity raises at least two important problems concerning selectivity. For one thing, in terms of what criteria are interpretations to be selected? For another, what are they to be selected as (e.g., as correct interpretations, plausible interpretations, etc.)? Construing the commas in (i) as "or" is, in a sense, already to take a significant step towards an answer to question (I) of form (ii), for it introduces into an understanding of interpretations a radical dissimilarity: it implies that not all interpretations are to be viewed as equally acceptable.

There is yet a further difficulty with an answer of form (i). The situation of interpretive diversity is by no means rare, where, for one reason or another, the one and the same text is given differing interpretations by their interpreters.[15] Scholarship in the humanities is familiar with this facet of research. Such diversity, however, raises profound meta-interpretive problems concerning what constitutes textual meaning, how this can be discerned, and whether or not the search for one and only one interpretation of a text is even legitimate, let alone feasible. Historicity, the kinds of questions the interpreter asks of a text, the tradition within which the interpreter stands, intentional textual ambiguity, etc., have all been cited as diversity-producing factors.

The meta-interpretive situation before us now, however, is of a different sort: not only is there diversity in meaning, there is interpretive conflict. The conclusions of two of the interpretive arguments are incompatible, two interpretations being incompatible when both cannot be true.[16] The conclusion of argument B is, for example, completely at odds with the conclusion of argument A. For A, the play represents an affirmation of the traditional religious outlook; for B, on the other hand, it is an exemplification of the valor and cost of inquiry. It cannot be the case that both are correct, and one cannot therefore accept both conclusions. Similarly, the conclusion of argument D stands opposed to any view of Oedipus which would make him out to be truly ignorant of his true identity at the outset of the play (as both premise A5 and premise B1 would appear to indicate).

The incompatibility goes even farther, as a comparison of arguments A and B would indicate. It does not lie in premises A1, A2, A3 or A4 which, on the whole, in no way conflict with the central points in argument B (although "catastrophe" in A4, unless a technical term, might be construed by A as too strong a word). Clearly premises A6 and B3 are at odds, for each see Oedipus as being like a different sort of person in Sophocles' own day. Why this is so rests on a further point of incompatibility; B1 and B2 are incompatible with A5. Both set out a different understanding of what Oedipus himself undergoes in the play.

The situation of interpretive incompatibility poses yet another problem for understanding an answer of form (i) to question (I). Are we therefore to understand by an answer of this sort that all interpretations, even incompatible ones, are to be accepted? This view would be congruent with the position that regards an answer of form (i) as all one can expect to question (I). It is also congruent with the view that regards the commas in (i) as "and." It is a view, however, that poses considerable problems of its own concerning what could be meant by "incompatibility" in such a context and how two or more "incompatible" interpretations could be simultaneously entertained by any one truth-regarding and truth-abiding individual. On the other hand, perhaps an answer of form (i) to question (I) should be regarded as again implying a

*Interpretation, Meta-Interpretation and Sophocles'* . . .

principle of selectivity, whereby one of the incompatible interpretations would be selected (and the others rejected), or else all rejected, but not where all incompatible interpretations would be accepted.

An answer of form (i) to question (I) raises, then, some intricate puzzles. Three important ones have been cited:

(1) how (i) is to be construed as an answer to question (I)

(2) how the commas in (i) are to be construed

(3) how the situation is to be understood whereby one interpretation (say) $i_x$ is incompatible with another interpretation (say $i_y$) of the same text.

If we stay simply on the level of interpretation we shall be stymied in our attempts to unravel these matters. We must move, then, to a meta-interpretive level so as to reflect on and hopefully understand better the interpretive situation before us. We have a text; we have several quite different, even incompatible, interpretations offered of it. What are we to make of this situation? I shall call this "question (II)." Put more formally, (II) is as follows:

(II) What are we to make of the situation whereby the question, "what does text t mean?" receives as an answer a reply of the following form: "text t means interpretation $i_1$, interpretation $i_2$, ..., interpretation $i_n$"?

Question (II) is an important, primary meta-interpretive question. In what follows I shall explore a few aspects of interpretive controversy that shed some light on unravelling the complex nature of question (II).

## 5. The Virtue of Interpretive Practice

It is important to note that we have come to question (II) out of an interpretive controversy in which the meaning of a text is disputed. This disputative aspect of textual interpretation is significant, and much overlooked. In a sense, an answer of form (i) to question (I) is apt to mislead us into thinking that we simply have a text and a series of alternative interpretations. While important, this is only one part of the contentious nature of textual interpretation. The matter is much more complex. It is not that interpreter $_1$ says "t means $i_1$"; interpreter $_2$ says "t means $i_2$"; and so on, as a series of alternative edicts or pronouncements upon the text's meaning. This understanding of the situation would ignore a substantial element in the disputative character of textual interpretation.

An interpreter does not just focus on a text: he attends also to other interpretations of the same text. In so doing, he develops and presents his own interpretation in the context of other understandings of the same text. He does not simply say "t means $i_x$." Rather the situation should be visualized schematically more along these lines:

> interpreter1 says "t means $i_1$"; interpreter $_2$, on the other hand, says, "No, it does not; t means $i_2$."

The "No, it does not" part is significant, for it serves to indicate an additional dimension of the controversial, contentious, and argumentative nature of textual interpretation.

Knox, for example, in working out what we have called "argument A," rejects Aristotle's view of the play (see premise A4) as well as all interpretive positions that regard the play as a tragedy of fate (see A1). Argument B rejects Knox's view of the process Oedipus undergoes in the play (see B3). Argument D rejects the position presupposed in arguments A (see A5) and B (see B1) that

Oedipus is not aware of his real identity at the play's beginning (see D2). Argument C, moreover, stands opposed to all interpretations (such as arguments A, B, and D) which focus exclusively on what Oedipus undergoes in the play to the total neglect of Jocasta. More could have been made out of this aspect of interpretation in our reconstruction of arguments A, B, C, and D, to show not only how interpretive positions are presented but also how they are advanced against other rival candidates in the field. In presenting a major interpretive argument there is usually a host of associated, subsidiary arguments. Enough has been said, however, to show that interpretation is worked out, not just by examining the text, but also by glancing sideways at the results of other interpretive efforts.

Textual interpretation is controversial, then, not just because a text has a series of different interpretations but also because these interpretations compete with one another. This aspect of textual interpretation presents some interesting features.

## Five Models of Interpretation

For one thing, the controversial nature of interpretation indicates certain basic structural features with which the study of interpretation should be concerned. These can be described in a series of models — models which serve to focus on the main structural elements of textual interpretation and which are useful in indicating the theoretical concerns raised by each sort of model.[17]

Frequently textual interpretation has been treated simply as a triadic relationship. This can be variously put, depending on what one thinks an interpreter does with a text when interpreting it. On one version,

    (1)   an interpreter provides (2) an interpretation of (3) a text.

He interprets it so as to come up with a statement of its meaning.[18] On another version,

>    (1)  an interpreter gives (2) an interpretation to (3) a text.[19]

The second formulation, while more colloquial, seems to close, or at least to limit, the possibility of reciprocity when interpreter meets text.

However the triadic model be phrased, it provides a framework for discussing textual interpretation. It also sets attention on some particular meta-interpretive matters:

>    (1)  how the three elements in the relationship function, separately and in interaction;
>
>    (2)  what the interpreter must take into account when providing/giving an interpretation of/to a text;
>
>    (3)  how the "providing of an interpretation" relates to the "giving of an interpretation to" a text;
>
>    (4)  the characteristics of the interpreter that impinge on textual interpretation (e.g., historicity, presuppositions, "horizon", etc.);
>
>    (5)  characteristics of the text that impinge on interpretation (e.g., its general linguistic character, authorship, its edited nature [if applicable], its provenance, etc.;

> (6) how the third element (*i.e.* texts) relates (if at all) to other items which interpreters are said to interpret (e.g., works of art, events, persons, etc.);

and so on. What is often overlooked in these discussions, however, is the relationship of element (2) to element (3), *i.e.*, of interpretation to text. What criteria must what is said about a text satisfy in order to count as an interpretation of that text? After all, not everything that can be said about a text constitutes an interpretation of that text.

Certainly these three elements, their nature and their various interrelationships, are essential to any understanding of textual interpretation. The questions this model poses remain fundamental for all additional models, although the matter grows increasingly more intricate as additional elements are added.

Some have added to the complexity by adding a fourth element. Bultmann (and others) have added the "for whom" an interpretation is provided, the logical model here being tetradic in kind:

> (1) an interpreter provides (2) an interpretation of (3) a text for (4) someone.

(Call this "someone" the "interpretation-recipient.") On this model, then, the interpreter is seen as a kind of mediator, one who stands between the text and the interpretation-recipient so as to present its meaning (with all its vitality and impact) to him (in terms he can comprehend). The process of demythologizing is one proposal for accomplishing the task of interpretative mediation for at least one sort of text.[20]

As is readily evident, a tetradic model opens up a new series of questions, as the interrelationships between the four elements are examined. The exigencies of the designated interpretation-recipients, and the interpreter's understanding of them, seem to play a role in what the interpreter has to do to/with a text so as to present its meaning to them. Indeed its meaning becomes enormously complicated, for, on this model, the meaning is not simply its meaning, nor even its meaning as interpreted by the interpreter (in terms he can grasp), but rather its meaning as interpreted by the interpreter in terms he thinks the interpretation-recipient can grasp. The transformations proposed here are immensely complex.

Another quite different tetradic model arises out of an appreciation of the "by whom" texts are written, thus adding the author as a fourth element:

(1) An interpreter provides (2) an interpretation of (3) a text which (4) an author has composed.

Both Dilthey and Hirsch have stressed this fourth element, although in quite different ways. This model again focuses inquiry in a specific direction, as the interrelationships between the author and the other three elements are explored. Questions arise concerning the necessity, desirability, and possibility of affinities between interpreter and author, and the bearing this may have on the understanding of the text. Questions arise, moreover, concerning the role of the author's intended meaning, access to it, and its relevance to the interpretation of the text. Other questions concern the absence of the fourth element in any perspicuous way for many sorts of texts, notably many myths, epics and sagas whose authorship cannot now be indicated.

Both tetradic models could conceivably be combined into a pentadic model, incorporating both the "for whom" and the "by whom" a text is written. I will not pursue this fourth model here but will turn instead to another sort of model in some greater detail.

Both the triadic and the two tetradic models mentioned ignore an important dimension of the interpretation of texts, namely its highly controversial aspect.

*Interpretation, Meta-Interpretation and Sophocles'...* 191

Interpreters do not just provide interpretations of texts, whether additionally for someone or in explicit recognition of the author by whom it came into being. They do so usually in the context of other interpreters having interpreted the same text and having done so differently, differently, that is, from each other and differently from the one the interpreter himself is about to provide. As has already been mentioned, interpreters interpret, not only in interaction with the text, but in full cognizance of other interpreters and interpretations of the same text. This points to a pentadic model of textual interpretation:

> (1) an interpreter provides (2) an interpretation of (3) a text in the context of (4) other interpreters who have provided (5) their interpretations of the same text.

As this pentadic model indicates, interpretations are not just provided. They are presented in the context of contentiousness in which they have to vie for existence with other different conflicting interpretive positions regarding the same text. In a word, they must fend for themselves in a hostile environment.

The triadic model, even augmented by author or interpretation-recipients, or both, represents a too restrictive, too private, even perhaps too friendly a view of textual interpretation. Interpretation is strife-ridden. The particular interpretive controversy we examined exemplified this; it is a situation which represents the usual circumstance in which the scholarly interpretation of texts, be they literary, legal, philosophical, religious, historical, *etc.*, proceeds.

Each model has hitherto served to shift the focus of inquiry in a specific direction. The same is true of this pentadic model as the five elements are viewed in their various interrelationships. A number of questions emerge. For one thing, how are the relationships between the various interpretations of the same text to be understood? Where, how, and why do they differ? And of what significance are their differences? For another thing, how does the interpretation the interpreter is proposing relate to prior interpretations? How does it get "established"? Moreover, how do all these competing interpretations relate to the text of which they are (putatively) interpretations? Are they all equally "interpretations of the text"? Are they to be spoken of in terms of correctness, or ranked according to some scale and conception of merit, or viewed as "plausible", or deemed acceptable as interpretations as "interesting" or "challenging" or "perceptive" comments on the text, *etc.*?

In other words, on this model, the questions that are thrust into prominence are ones that concern how interpretations relate to each other and to the text. Ultimately this model throws open the more radical questions — what is a text, if it be such as to permit so many divergent interpretations of itself? Indeed, what is it to be an interpretation of a text? In what relation must it stand to the text?

This pentadic model, one suggested by and congruent with the controversial nature of interpretation, has received scant attention.

### Interpretive Reasons

In addition to the pentadic structure of interpretation, there is another meta-interpretive aspect that arises from an explicit acknowledgement of the disputative character of interpretation. It should be apparent that the answer to question (I) is considerably more complex than the answer of form (i) would indicate. The answer given to question (I) is not just that the text means this or that interpretation. Rather the answer takes the form that the text means such-and-such for such-and-such reasons. This is readily evident from the interpretive controversy we examined: in each case the interpreters in arguments, A, B, C, and D backed up their interpretive position with reasons. Put schematically, the answer to question (I) takes the following form:

(iii) text t means interpretation $i_x$ because... (and here a variety of reasons are cited).

In other words, interpretations are not simply given. They are justified, defended, and argued for. Interpretive positions come equipped with interpretive reasons.

Interpreting, then, in the context of controversy, has the following specific structure: an interpretive position supported by a variety of interpretive reasons. The structure is important, for it indicates a direction. However interpretations are discovered (and here, surely, many factors play a prominent role: creativity, insight, scholarly abilities, *etc.*), when they are offered on the public stage as interpretations, they are presented with the full understanding that they need to be established or justified. It is recognized that an interpretation will be inspected not only in relation to the text of which it is an interpretation, but also in relation to other interpretations of the same text of which it is a rival. As a result, interpretations can never be edicts or proclamations of a text's meaning. Because of what an interpretation must do — express the text's meaning in an arena in which other competing interpretive efforts aim to do precisely that — it has quite a different character.

### Interpretive Arguments

In recognizing that interpretive positions come equipped with interpretive reasons, we have thereby acknowledged that interpretations are presented in the format of interpretive arguments. This is the form of interpretation — not edicts, pronouncements, proclamations, or any other form of sheer assertiveness that such-and such is the case. Interpretations exhibit all the common features of arguments: conclusions (*i.e.*, the interpretive position), premises (*i.e.*, the interpretive reasons), and support for the individual premises — indeed, the whole panoply of "main arguments" and "mini-arguments" which make up the fabric of disputation.[21] This is a significant aspect of interpretation, one that has been overlooked, although it has always been before us, in interpretative practice. Argument is the mode of interpretation.

Recognition of this form is important to meta-interpretive inquiry. For one thing, it is instrumental in value. It helps to pinpoint key claims, to organize supporting considerations, to show on what grounds an interpretive position is advanced, to indicate how an interpretive position is defended, and so on. Good interpretive practice has always reflected this. It has, in addition, significant theoretical import.

Recognition of the argumentive form of textual interpretation enables us, moreover, to differentiate between the *interpretive result* (*i.e.*, the conclusion of the interpretive argument) and the *interpretive reasons* (*i.e.*, the premises of the interpretive argument). This distinction is important, for the claim that many texts are such that they are capable of receiving diverse, differing, or conflicting interpretations is imprecise. Wherein they differ is crucial. Interpretations that differ do differ not only in interpretive result but also in interpretive reasons. This approach, therefore, has the advantage of readily locating wherein disputes lie.

Thirdly, recognition of the argumentative form of textual interpretation also makes clear the basis on which differing interpretive results differ — *i.e.*, in the premises which constitute their respective lines of reasoning. In examining interpretive disputes from a meta-interpretive perspective, this has the thrust of transferring hermeneutic attention away from the obvious discrepancy (two or more diverse or conflicting interpretive conclusions) to what is more subtle and complex (the divergent interpretive reasons). By these means, points of agreement and disagreement can be readily singled out, as was done, for instance, in section IV of this paper for arguments A, B, C, and D. This shift to differing interpretive reasons constitutes an important step in the meta-interpretive investigation of interpretive disputes.

Fourthly, once the meta-interpretive focus has shifted to the reasons for an interpretive conclusion, then the matter becomes one of judging which interpretive premises are well or better defended by supporting considerations. It puts the onus on the interpreters to defend their interpretive reasons and to challenge the differing interpretive reasons of others — *by the evidence*. The hermeneutic shift, then, is not simply to the interpretive premises as such but to the supporting considerations that underlie each premise that plays an important role in the interpretive dispute in question. In the dispute concerning arguments A and B on the meaning of *Oedipus Tyrannus*, for instance, meta-interpretive focus should properly be placed on the reasons that support A5 on the one hand versus the reasons that support B1 and B2 on the other, for that is what is at issue.

In essence this approach has the enormous theoretical import of taking meta-interpretive emphasis away from the *persons involved* — the focus on the author and the interpreter so prevalent in various forms of hermeneutics of the post-Schleiermacher period — and placing it upon *the relationship between what is said about a text by way of interpreting it and the text itself*. This relationship, the one between the interpretation (*i.e.*, interpretive conclusion and interpretive premises) and the text itself, is what should bear the brunt of meta-interpretive scrutiny. This places hermeneutics directly in the same sort of square of controversy in which other kinds of disputes — *e.g.*, legal, academic, scientific, moral, governmental, *etc.* — find expression, challenge, and perhaps eventual resolution.

This makes explicit that interpretations are texts written about texts. What is being compared are the contents of scraps of paper: the text, an interpretation, other interpretations of the same text. The thrust of this approach — indeed, that of the whole pentadic model of textual interpretation — is simply to make central in meta-interpretive inquiry how these elements relate. How must the interpreting writing relate to the interpreted text so that the former constitutes an interpretation of the latter? And how do two or more interpreting writings relate to one another? These two questions now become the pivotal ones in meta-interpretation.

This is not the place to work out a full-scale study of interpretive arguments. A study of this sort would systematically examine some representative kinds of interpretive arguments, culled from a detailed analysis of good interpretive practice. It would note how interpretations are advanced, how they are defended, how and wherein interpretations of the same text differ, what kinds of evidence are introduced in establishing an interpretive conclusion, what kinds of evidence are rejects or modified in the course of an interpretive controversy, how other interpretations are argued against, and so forth. The study would focus on the sorts of evidence interpretive arguments typically cite.

Such a study is clearly well beyond the perimeters of this paper. It is important, however, to see that such a study is the meta-interpretive direction that attention to the features of interpretive controversy places before us. Nor is this the appropriate place to work out a "logic" of textual interpretation, although, I submit, it is in this direction that such a logic is to be found. A logic of textual interpretation would be a logic of interpretive arguments. Nor is this the place to work out a hermeneutics of fidelity. I suggest, however, that it is in this direction that such a hermeneutics is to be found, in working out and assessing the interpretation that is best supported by the text, *i.e.*, in ascertaining the best interpretive argument for that text.

This meta-interpretive approach raises some important problems, however. For example, for one thing, how should the relationship between interpretation and text be characterized? This question needs answering so as to enable us to distinguish between comments made about a text that constitute genuine interpretations of that text from those comments that fail to be. For another, when ought an interpretive claim (either conclusion or premise) be said to be "well supported" or adequately defended by a text? The relation of textual interpretation to its textual evidential base needs to be made clear if the notion of "being faithful to" the text is to have precise meaning. And, thirdly, what kinds of evidence are evidence for the truth of interpretive claims. Should we admit, for example, as a fundamental meta-interpretive principle, the position that

> unless there is good reason to the contrary, the primary evidence for the truth of an interpretive claim is textual evidence?

Such a meta-interpretive "rule of evidence" would rule out as evidence for an interpretation such considerations as information about the author, about extra-textual contexts (such as, of its first having been written, of its transmission, of its being read today), and of the interpreter, etc., unless good reasons are cited by the interpreter for admitting such evidence into the discussion.

Citing these important problems is not to admit defeat. Rather it is to suggest, on the basis of the meta-interpretive approach advocated here, the proper location of hermeneutic inquiry. It is also to point out that in this inquiry, meta-interpretation is not alone. The relation of claim to evidence is a central problem in any area of endeavor in which disputes are investigated by argument.

### ... Meaning ...: Some qualifications

Interpretive arguments seek to establish what a text means. This involves argumentation on two fronts. First of all, in relation to the text itself, it involves an argument whose conclusion is of the following form:

> Therefore: t means $i_x$.

Secondly, in relation to other interpretations of the same text, the interpretation has to establish itself as an interpretation — to look after its own credentials, as it were. This involves an associated argument (or arguments) whose conclusion(s) is of the following form:

> Therefore: t does not mean $i_y$, $i_z$, etc. (where $i_y$, $i_z$, etc. have been advanced as interpretations of the text by other interpreters).

Interpretive arguments, then, argue both what a text means and (at least with respect to some other interpretations offered of the same text) what it does not mean. This was evident in our presentation of arguments A, B, C, and D in sections 2 and 3 above and in the analysis of their various points of disagreement in section 4.

Interpretive arguments provide the way in which question (I) is answered. How they answer question (I), however, is important, for they indicate a basic lack of clarity about the question itself that needs now to be noted. The "means" in question (I), and in the answer to question (i), needs to be qualified in certain ways. One way of accomplishing this is as follows.

In reading the Book of Job, for instance, an interpreter might hazard the interesting interpretive guess that contrary to one usual line of interpretation that regards the work as about Job and his suffering, the work is really about God and the Covenant, a work that really probes two main issues: (1) whether life lived within the Covenantal relationship is really a blessed life, and (2) whether there is any assurance that God himself is honoring the Covenant. Seen in this light, the Book of Job would represent a refreshing reappraisal of, perhaps even a sharp corrective to, prophetic edicts on these matters. This interpreter has not yet worked out the details of this line of interpretation — *i.e.*, he has not yet formulated an interpretive argument. He has simply indicated his impression of what the work *might mean*.

In this case, the work might mean this, although, of course, it might not. We would have to wait and see, to await, in other words, the formulation and presentation of an interpretive argument on behalf of the interpretive position being advanced, and judge it by the evidence it presents in its defense. As it stands, the view simply represents one possibility, one interesting interpretive avenue to explore. There is nothing very definite, nothing very settled, about this interpretive hunch. It is simply a possibility, a consideration for future study.

A claim that a text t *might mean* such-and-such is simply the statement of an interpretive suggestion, one that admits of many alternative possibilities, and one that remains to be tested by a closer examination of textual evidence. On the other hand, an interpreter might be somewhat more definite about what a text means. An interpreter may be examining the Book of Daniel. For a variety of reasons, and from a close examination of the text, he may have at least provisionally accepted (1) that the work was initially composed *ca.* 167-164 B.C., and (2) that its provenance is the resistance movement of the Hasidim. This may suggest to him that at least chapters 1 through 6 of this work may very well have an allegorical meaning, one that equates Nebuchadnezzar with Antiochus Ephiphanes and which also identifies the incidents or situations in chapters 1 through 6 (allegedly from Nebuchadnezzar's time) with incidents or situations in the time of Antiochus Ephiphanes. The work may very well present an analysis, in code or allegorical form, of the predicament with which the Hasidim were faced.

The work may very well mean this — at least some evidence suggests that it is a fruitful avenue to explore. It all depends on whether or not the proposed equations hold up, how one relates Chapters 1 through 6 with the remaining chapters of the work (a problem of unity), and so forth. It, of course, may very well not mean this at all. Only a fuller exploration of the text will tell. As it stands, it is an interpretation taking shape: textual matters are being explored and an interpretive argument is in the making.

A claim that a text t may very well mean such-and-such is one that indicates that an interpretive position has some evidence to support it and that further evidence could be or is being gathered to develop it fully. It is not yet a full-blown interpretive argument. It has promise (promise because of evidence, it should be noted).

An interpretive argument is offered, however, when things have gelled — when puzzles in the text, when problems and difficulties in other interpretations of the text, when niggles in one's own understanding of the text have been ironed out. It is an account that emerges when everything "fits," when the pieces come together in a cohesive fashion. An interpretive argument therefore takes shape when the interpreter has "settled" on an interpretation of the text. It represents what the interpreter contends the text *must mean* — must mean, that is, according to the evidence taken into account. Interpretive arguments in positions A, B, C, and D are of this nature. They represent "settled" views of what the text must mean. Each is offered as an expression of what the text has to mean, given the textual evidence consulted, and each is ready to do battle and match wits with other interpretive positions.

A claim that a text t must mean such-and-such is one that indicates that an interpretive argument has been formulated and that an interpretation of the text has been settled upon. The interpretation is, of course, open to revision — revision, that is, in accordance with new evidence or reassessment of old evidence. Such an interpretation is not offered as one of many: it is offered as the text's interpretation.

Question (I), then, should be understood in at least three different senses, depending on how "means" is qualified. So regarded, question (I) may be asking any of the following questions:

(a) what *might* text t *mean*?
(b) what *may* text t very well *mean*?
(c) what *must* text t *mean*?

These are quite different questions, and they call for quite different answers. The answer to question (I) in terms of what a text might mean will be very different from an answer either in terms of what it may very well mean or what it must mean. For one thing, the amount of evidential support one would expect the answer to provide would vary in each instance.

An answer of the form, text t means ix because ... (where a variety of reasons are cited) is an answer that provides an interpretive argument, one that thereby indicates a settled interpretation of the text. It is an answer, therefore, to question (I) construed as asking, what must text t mean? It is not presented as one in a series of possible meanings not yet fully thought out.

It is for this reason that we can now go back to an answer of form (i) to question (I), a form that posed many interpretive difficulties of its own. I indicated some time ago that some would argue that such an answer is unresponsive. This contention is well-founded, for a reason that is now apparent. For to ask question (I) and to receive in reply one or more interpretive arguments is to be confronted with the question in its must-mean sense. To a question that asks, what must text t mean? It would be unresponsive to answer, it means $i_1, i_2,...,i_n$, for the answer is cast in might-mean or may-very-well-mean terms, senses of "means" that admit of alternative interpretive possibilities.

### Incompatible Interpretations

If we understand question (I) as asking what must text t mean? and if we understand interpretive arguments as serious attempts to provide an answer to that question, then certain important consequences follow. For one thing, we would not say that an answer of form (i) to question (I) is all we can expect, for that is precisely the sort of answer we would not expect to the question as so understood. Such an answer would not only not be informative: it would also not be an answer to that question. Secondly, one would therefore not construe the commas in an answer of form (i) as "and" but rather as exclusive "or." One could not remain content with a simple listing of possible meaning. Some selection is indicated. Thirdly, an answer of form (ii) would seem to be more in keeping with question (i) as so understood, although the route to that answer is now seen to be complicated. Selection among rival interpretations would involve the judging of the range of interpretive arguments offered of the text in question, in keeping with the ways in which arguments generally are assessed and in keeping also with any peculiarities concerning interpretive evidence that a detailed study of interpretive arguments may unearth.

This is clearly the case for incompatible interpretations. Where two interpretations of one and the same text are incompatible, say $i_x$ and $i_y$, there are three possible answers:

(1) neither $i_x$ nor iy is correct (but another one, namely $i_j$, is).

(2) one of $i_x$ and $i_y$ is correct, namely....

(3) no interpretation is correct because the text is such that it lacks any one clear meaning.

but not

(4) both $i_x$ and $i_y$ are correct.

(4) is ruled out in the case of incompatibility, for by definition, it cannot be the case that both can be true. We cannot, in this case, appeal either to the richness

of the text or to the fecundity of the interpreter's wit and imagination to license interpretive diversity.

Moreover, in the situation of Sophocles' *Oedipus Tyrannus* where two incompatible interpretations are available [namely, the conclusions of arguments A and B], (3) cannot be the case. Options (1) and (2) are the only ones open. In either instance, however, the matter involves settling upon the interpretation of the text, selecting one over others. The method of that selection has already been indicated.

The situation is the same for all rival interpretations of the same text, all interpretations, that is, that present interpretive arguments in response to question (I) understood as asking what text t must mean. The task of interpretive selection cannot be avoided in this instance.

## 6. In Sum

Three things have been done in this article. We have surveyed several different interpretations of Sophocles' *Oedipus Tyrannus* (including one new one) as an example of an interpretive controversy; we have scouted out a meta-interpretive direction, one that acknowledges the disputative character of textual interpretation; and we have scrutinized several significant ramifications of this, noting, in particular, a pentadic model of interpretation and the central role of interpretive arguments in the study of meta-interpretation. We used interpretations of Sophocles' *Oedipus Tyrannus* to open up a different meta-interpretive direction, thus demonstrating the virtue of interpretive practice.

The paper began with a quotation from Jocasta who accuses two arguers — Oedipus and Creon — with having raised a foolish war of words. Interpretation is a war of words (although no foolish one) and it is this aspect on which we have focused. We have, for the most part, been writing about writing about texts. We never did answer our initial question, what does

Sophocles' *Oedipus Tyrannus* mean? But perhaps now we have a sense of what that question means, what some of its complexities involve, and a notion of a direction in which an answer may be found.

## ENDNOTES

[1] For a discussion of different conceptions of hermeneutics, see Richard E. Palmer, *Hermeneutics* (Evanston: Northwestern University Press 1969) chaps. 3 & 5.

[2] Bernard M. W. Knox, *Oedipus at Thebes* (New York: W. W. Norton 1971). All subsequent references to this work (first published in 1957 by Yale University Press) will be to the Norton edition and will be placed in parentheses following the quoted or referred-to material.

[3] The following works by Rudolf Bultmann are pertinent in this respect: "New Testament and Mythology," in. W. Bartsch (ed.), *Kerygma and Myth*, I (London: S.P.C.K. 1964) 1-44; "The Problem of Hermeneutics," in R. Bultmann, *Essays Philosophical and Theological* (London; SCM Press, 1955) 234-61; *Jesus Christ and Mythology* (New York: Scribner's, 1958); and "Is Exegesis without Presuppositions Possible?" in *Existence and Faith: Shorter Writings of Rudolf Bultmann*, trans. Schubert M. Ogden (New York: World, 1960). For a critical discussion of Bultmann's position, see, for instance, the author's "Bultmann's Hermeneutics; A Critical Examination," *International Journal for Philosophy of Religion* 8 (1977), 169-89 [reprinted in this volume].

[4] See, for instance, the following works by Hans-Georg Gadamer: *Le Problème de la Conscience Historique* (Paris: Béatrice-Nauwelaerts, 1963); *Truth and Method* (New York: Seabury, 1975. Originally published as *Wahrheit und Methode* (Tübingen: 1965); and *Philosophical Hermeneutics* (Berkeley and Los Angeles: University of California Press, 1976).

[5] Among a great many authors, the now classic works of Dilthey, Heidegger, and Ebeling should especially be mentioned. See also R. E. Palmer, *op.cit.*; Robert R. Magliola, *Phenomenology and Literature* (West Lafayette: Purdue University Press, 1977); and David Couzens Hoy, *The Critical Circle* (Berkeley and Los Angeles: University of California Press, 1978).

[6] See E.D. Hirsch, Jr., *Validity in Interpretation* (New Haven: Yale University Press 1967), and *Aims of Interpretation* (Chicago: University of Chicago Press 1976). For a critical discussion of Hirsch's position, see, for instance, the author's "Hirsch's Hermeneutics: A Critical Examination," *Philosophy Today* 22 (1978) 29-33 [reprinted in this volume].

[7] Oscar Cullmann, *The Christology of the New Testament* (Philadelphia: Westminster, 1959) xiv. See also "Les problèmes posés par la méthode exégetique de l'école de Karl Barth," *Revue d'Histoire et de Philosophie Religieuses* 8 (1928), 70-83.

[8] It should be pointed out here that I am not a classics scholar but rather a philosopher interested in the works of classical antiquity. In my study of the play I have consulted the following: F. Storr (trans.), *Sophocles: Oedipus the King* (London: William Heinemann, Loeb Classical Library, 1912); Bernard M. W. Knox, *op. cit.*; Thomas Gould (trans., with commentary), *Sophocles, Oedipus the King* (Englewood Cliffs: Prentice-Hall, 1970); Luci Berkowitz and Theodore F. Brunner (trans., ed.), *Sophocles, Oedipus Tyrannus* (New York: W. W. Norton, 1970); and Philip Vellacott, *Sophocles and Oedipus* (Ann Arbor: University of Michigan Press, 1971).

[9] As Knox puts it (pp. 46, 47), the argument in the play runs as follows: (1) if the prophecy given to Laius does not correspond with reality, then prophecy is false. (2) But that prophecy does correspond with reality. Therefore prophecy is not false. This, however, is an invalid argument (fallacy of denying the antecedent). It is perhaps better to rephrase the first premise, if prophecy is false then the prophecy given to Laius does not correspond with reality, for this seems to make better sense and would lead validly to the desired conclusion.

[10] Perhaps there is a connection between this question and Oedipus' initial question, for the oracle, knowing Oedipus' character, might correctly assume that Oedipus, on hearing the answer to this question, would construe it as an answer to the question concerning what he should do to relieve the city's plight.

[11] Parmenides, *Way of Truth*. Selection 6.10 in John Manley Robinson, *An Introduction to Early Greek Philosophy* (Boston: Houghton Mifflin, 1968) 113.

[12] Cf. the discussion between Socrates and Meno, *Meno* 97a-99a; cf. also the discussion between Awida and Bardaisan in *The Book of the Laws of the Countries*, trans. H.J.W. Drijvers (Assen: Van Gorcum, 1965) 7-9.

[13] *Republic* 514A-521B.

[14] Philip Vellacott, *op. cit.* References to this work in Argument D are placed in parentheses following the quoted or referred-to material.

*Interpretation, Meta-Interpretation and Sophocles'...* 207

[15]Note, for instance, the interpretive controversy concerning the meaning of Shakespeare's *Hamlet*: Morris Weitz, *Hamlet and the Philosophy of Literary Criticism* (Chicago: University of Chicago Press, 1964); Paul Gottschalk, *The Meanings of Hamlet* (Albuquerque: University of New Mexico Press, 1972). Consider also the interpretive controversy concerning the interpretation of the parables of Jesus: see, for instance, Dan Otta Via, Jr., *The Parables* (Philadelphia: Fortress, 1967); John Dominic Crossan, *In Parables* (New York: Harper & Row, 1973); Norman Perrin, *Jesus and the Language of the Kingdom* (Philadelphia: Fortress, 1976); etc.

[16]The topic of incompatible interpretations of a work has received some attention in a number of works, although it has not always been made clear under what circumstances one interpretation is said to be "incompatible" with another. See, for instance, the following studies which touch, at least in part, on the topic of incompatible interpretations: Joseph Margolis, "The Logic of Interpretation," in Margolis, *The Language of Art and Art Criticism* (Detroit: Wayne State University Press, 1965); Monroe C. Beardsley, *The Possibility of Criticism* (Detroit: Wayne State University Press, 1970); Denis Dutton, "Plausibility and Aesthetic Interpretation," *Canadian Journal of Philosophy* 7 (1977), 327-40; Joseph Margolis, "Robust Relativism," in Margolis (ed.), *Philosophy Looks at the Arts* (Philadelphia: Temple University Press, 1978); and John Reichert, *Making Sense of Literature* (Chicago: University of Chicago Press, 1978). See also Jack W. Meiland, "Interpretation as a Cognitive Discipline," *Philosophy and Literature* 2 (1978), 23-45, which discusses multiple interpretations of the same text.

[17]For my use of 'model,' see Max Black, *Models and Metaphors* (Ithaca: Cornell University Press, 1962); Mary B. Hesse, *Models and Analogies in Science* (London: Sheed and Ward, 1963); and Ian T. Ramsey, *Models and Mystery* (London: Oxford University Press, 1964).

[18]Cf. Beardsley, *op. cit.*, who describes (literary) interpretation in the following way: "...any such statement, or set of statements, used to report discovered meaning in a literary text I shall call a "literary interpretation" (p. 38). In an earlier work, Beardsley had described interpretation as verbally unfolding or disclosing meaning. See his "The Limits of Critical Interpretation," in Sidney Hook (ed.), Art and Philosophy (New York: New York University Press 1966) 61-87. This view is strongly criticized by Joseph Margolis, "Three Problems in Aesthetics," in Sidney Hook, op. cit., 262-70.

[19]Cf. Margolis' distinction between describing and interpreting. The latter suggests "...a touch of virtuosity, an element of performance, a shift from a stable object whose properties, however complex, are simply enumerable to an object

whose properties pose something of a puzzle or a challenge — with emphasis on the solution of the puzzle, or on some inventive use of the materials present, on the added contribution of the interpreter, and on a certain openness toward possible alternative interpretations." See "Describing and Interpreting Works of Art," in Margolis, *The Language of Art and Art Criticism* chap. 5.

[20] Allegorical hermeneutics — for example, of the sort proposed by Origen, John Cassian, or Augustine — represents another way of accomplishing interpretive mediation. On this approach, the interpreter relates the text's meaning to a variety of interpretive levels, depending on the interpretation-recipient's level of comprehension. The interpreter, moreover, on this approach also bears in mind when interpreting certain texts (*e.g.*, the Old Testament) the new reality in which the interpretation-recipient lives (*i.e.*, on the post-resurrection side of Jesus' life).

[21] This direction differs considerably from that suggested by Margolis in "The Logic of Interpretation," and from that indicated by Richard Shusterman, "The Logic of Interpretation," *Philosophical Quarterly* 28 (1978), 310-324.

# INDEX

Allegory, 15, 16, 208
Antiochene School, 23
Application, 18, 19
Aristotle, 4, 132, 166
Augustine, 16, 132
Bardaisan, 63, 82, 131-155
Barth, Karl, 63, 64, 75, 83
Bultmann, Rudolf, 59-85, 110, 160, 205
Calvin, 11
Cassian, 16
Cullmann, Oscar 64, 83, 161, 206
Daniel, Book of, 4, 197
Das Verstehen 37-45, 56, 57, 59
Demythologizing, 67-69, 71-81, 83-85
Descartes, 30
Dilthey, Wilhelm, v, vi, 3, 12, 17, 20, 22, 27-57, 59, 60, 65, 87, 190
Dilthey's Dilemma, 47-50
Downward Interpretive Spiral Vortex, 10, 20
Droysen, 38, 54, 55
Eliot, T.S., 3, 22, 99, 100, 112
European Metaphysical System, 29-31
Fichte, 33
Fusion of Horizons, 18, 19
Gadamer, Hans-Georg, 16-20, 21, 24, 110, 160
Hegel, 12, 28, 33
Heidegger, 12, 110
Hesiod, 15
Hirsch, Jr. E.D., 12-14, 23, 87-113, 160, 190, 205

Homer, 15
Hume, David, 30, 31
Husserl, 53, 103
Interpretive Arguments, 193-197
Interpretive Conflict, 181
Interpretive Diversity, 6, 181
Interpretive Incompatibility 181-183, 200, 201
Interpretive Practice, 183-185
Interpretive Reasons, 192-193
Job, Book of, 14, 198
Kant, 30, 33, 98, 111
Knox, Bernard, 159, 160, 163-170, 205, 206
Macquarrie, John, 75, 84, 85
Models of Interpretation, 187-191
Multiple Sense Approach, 7, 15
*Oedipus Tyrannus*, 159-181
Origen, 15, 16, 21
Palmer, Richard E., 23, 205
Plato, 4, 14, 63, 82, 98, 117-130, 178
Prejudice, 17, 18
Prior Understanding, 61-63
Protestant Reformation, 11, 12
St. Paul, 14
Schelling, 33
Schleiermacher, 12, 33, 38-41, 55, 56, 59, 60
Schopenhauer, 33
Shakespeare, 4, 23, 205
Single Sense Approach, 7, 17
Theory of Semantic Autonomy, 88-111
Vellacott, Philip, 179, 181
Xenophon, 119, 129

# PROBLEMS IN CONTEMPORARY PHILOSOPHY

1. Petra von Morstein, **On Understanding Works of Art: An Essay in Philosophical Aesthetics**

2. David and Randall Basinger, **Philosophy and Miracle: The Contemporary Debate**

3. Franscico Peccorini Letona, **Selfhood as Thinking Thought in the Work of Gabriel Marcel**

4. Corbin Fowler, **The Logic of U.S. Nuclear Weapons Policy: A Philosophical Analysis**

5. Marcus P. Ford (ed.), **A Process Theory of Medicine: Interdisciplinary Essays**

6. Lars Aagaard-Mogensen (ed.), **The Idea of the Museum: Philosophical, Artistic, and Political Questions**

7. Kerry S. Walters, **The Sane Society in Modern Utopianism: A Study in Ideology**

8. Steven W. Laycock, **Foundations for a Phenomenological Theology**

9. John R. Jacobson and Robert Lloyd Mitchell (eds.), **Existence of God: Essays from the Basic Issues Forum**

10. Richard J. Connell, **The Empirical Intelligence - The Human Empirical Mode: Philosophy As Originating in Experience**

11. Sander H. Lee (ed.), **Inquiries into Values: The Inaugural Session of the International Society for Value Inquiry**

12. Tobias Chapman, **In Defense of Mystical Ideas: Support for Mystic Beliefs from a Purely Theoretical Viewpoint**

13. Donald Stewart, **Entities and Individuation: Studies in Ontology and Language**

14. Peter Preuss, **Reincarnation**

15. Tibor R. Machan, **The Moral Case for the Free Market Economy: A Philosophical Argument**

16. George Frederick Schueler, **The Idea of a Reason for Acting: A Philosophical Argument**

17. William and Harriet Lovitt, **Modern Technology in the Heideggerian Perspective**

18. William Cooney (ed.), **Reflections on Gabriel Marcel: A Collection of Essays**

19. Mari Sorri and Jerry Gill, **A Post-Modern Epistemology: Language, Truth, and Body**

20. Adolf Portmann, **Essays in Philosophic Zoology:** *The Living Form and the Seeing Eye*, Richard B. Carter (trans.)

21. George Englebretson, **Essays on the Philosophy of Fred Sommers: In Logical Terms**

22. Kevin Doran, **What is a Person: The Concept and the Implications for Ethics**

23. Ronald Roblin (ed.), **The Aesthetics of the Critical Theorists: Studies on Benjamin, Adorno, Marcuse, and Habermas**

24. William Lane Craig and Mark S. McLeod (eds.), **The Logic of Rational Theism: Exploratory Essays**

25. Barrie A. Wilson, **Hermeneutical Studies: Dilthey, Sophocles, and Plato**

26. John D. Jones, **Poverty and the Human Condition: A Philosophical Inquiry**